All-in-One Bible Fun
Fruit of the Spirit
Elementary

Also available from Abingdon Press

All-in-One Bible Fun

Fruit of the Spirit
Preschool

Stories of Jesus
Preschool

Stories of Jesus
Elementary

Favorite Bible Stories
Preschool

Favorite Bible Stories
Elementary

Heroes of the Bible
Preschool

Heroes of the Bible
Elementary

Writers/Editors: LeeDell Stickler, Daphna Flegal
Production Editors: Billie Brownell, Anna Raitt
Production and Design Manager: Marcia C'deBaca
Illustrator: Megan Jeffery
Cover photo: jupiterimages

All-in-One

BIBLE

FUN

Fruit of the Spirit
Elementary

ABINGDON PRESS
Nashville

All-in-One BIBLE FUN
Table of Contents

Bible Units in *Fruit of the Spirit*

Use these suggestions if you choose to organize the lessons in short-term units.

Fruit of the Spirit

Bible Story	Bible Verse
Love	Love is patient; love is kind. 1 Corinthians 13:4
Joy	Sing for joy to the LORD, all the earth. Psalm 98:4, GNT
Peace	Blessed are the peacemakers, for they will be called children of God. Matthew 5:9
Patience	Be patient and wait for the LORD to act. Psalm 37:7, GNT
Kindness	The scripture says, "It is kindness that I want." Matthew 12:7, GNT
Generosity	For God loves a cheerful giver. 2 Corinthians 9:7
Faithfulness	Do everything God commands, and be faithful to God. Deuteronomy 11:22, GNT
Gentleness	Let your gentleness be known to everyone. Philippians 4:5
Self-control	Let us choose what is right. Job 34:4

Other Christian Virtues

Bible Story	Bible Verse
Honesty	Be honest and you show that you have reverence for the LORD. Proverbs 14:2, GNT
Forgiveness	You must forgive one another. Colossians 3:13, GNT
Obedience	For the love of God is this, that we obey God's commandments. 1 John 5:3, adapted
Responsibility	Let your light shine before others, so that they may see your good works. Matthew 5:16

Supplies

(This is a comprehensive list of all the supplies needed if you choose to do all the activities. It is your choice whether your group will do all the activities.)

- Bibles
- crayons
- pencils
- chalk
- plastic fruit
- plastic sandwich bags
- gum erasers
- plastic coins, real coins, or metal washers
- cowboy hats, bandannas, apron, ropes, western gear
- paper punch
- coffee cans or shortening cans
- plastic toy figure
- basket
- watercolor and permanent felt-tip markers
- construction paper
- index cards
- scissors
- masking tape and clear tape
- shallow bowls or dishes
- tempera paint, paint brushes
* smocks
- plastic sandwich bags
- newspaper
- white cloth, purple or blue cloth
- wooden toothpicks
- glass jars
- pinking shears
- neon acrylic poster paints
- rubber bands
- paper plates
- paper napkins
- stapler, staples
- table salt or sand
- string, yarn, ribbon

- paper cups
- white glue
- plastic dishpan, water
- examples of illuminated manuscripts
- drinking straws
- lunch-size paper bags
- cookies or crackers
- sticky notes
- drawing paper
- scarfs/blindfolds
- envelopes
- large paper grocery bags
- metal baking pan
- large-size paper
- balls
- sponges
- plain wrapping paper
- items that come in graduated sizes such as paper cups, paper plates, boxes
- crown, large book
- courtroom set up, gavel, robe for judge
- wooden pole
- a variety of potentially noisy items such as metal pots, pans, and lids; metal bowls; wooden spoons; empty soda cans; disposable aluminum pie pans
- clean-up supplies

Welcome to All-in-One Bible Fun

Have fun learning about the fruit of the Spirit. Each lesson in this teacher guide is filled with games and activities that will make learning fun for you and your children. With just a few added supplies, everything you need to teach is included in Abingdon's *All-in-One Bible Fun*. Each lesson has a box with a picture of a cookie,

Love is patient and kind.

that is repeated over and over again throughout the lesson. The cookie box states the Bible message in words your children will understand.

Use the following tips to help make *All-in-One Bible Fun* a success!

balloon symbol

- Read through each lesson. Read the Bible passages.
- Memorize the Bible verse and the cookie box statement.
- Choose activities that fit your unique group of children and your time limitations. If time is limited, we recommend those activities noted in **boldface** on the chart page and by a *balloon* beside each activity.
- Practice telling the Bible story.
- Gather supplies you will use for the lesson.
- Learn the music included in each lesson. All the songs are written to familiar tunes.
- Arrange your room space to fit the lesson. Move tables and chairs so there is plenty of room for the children to move and to sit on the floor.
- Copy the Reproducible pages for the lesson.

Elementary

Each child in your class is a one-of-a-kind child of God. Each child has his or her own name, background, family situation, and set of experiences. It is important to remember and celebrate the uniqueness of each child. Yet these one-of-a-kind children of God have some common needs.

- All children need love.
- All children need a sense of self-worth.
- All children need to feel a sense of accomplishment.
- All children need to have a safe place to be and express their feelings.
- All children need to be surrounded by adults who love them.
- All children need to experience the love of God.

Younger elementary children (ages 6-10 years old) also have some common characteristics.

Their Bodies

- They are growing at different rates.
- They are energetic, restless, and have difficulty sitting still.
- They are developing fine motor skills.
- They want to participate rather than watch or listen.

Their Minds

- They are developing basic academic skills.
- They are eager to learn new things.
- They learn best by working imaginatively and creatively.
- They have little sense of time.
- They are concrete thinkers and cannot interpret symbols.
- They are developing an ability to reason and discuss.
- They like to have a part in planning their own activities.

Their Relationships

- They want to play with other children.
- They are sensitive to the feelings of others.
- They are shifting dependence from parents to teachers.
- They enjoy team activities but often dispute the rules.
- They imitate adults in attitudes and actions.

Their Hearts

- They are open to learning about God.
- They need caring adults who model Christian behaviors.
- They need to sing, move to, and say Bible verses.
- They need to hear simple Bible stories.
- They can talk with God easily if encouraged.
- They are asking questions about God.
- They can share food and money and make things for others.

All-in-One
BIBLE ELEMENTARY
FUN

Love

Bible Verse

Love is patient; love is kind.

1 Corinthians 13:4

Bible Story

Galatians 5:22–23; 1 Corinthians 13

The term "fruit of the Spirit" comes from the idea that Christians grow in the faith, and this growth produces Christian virtues such as love and joy. The fruit of love is self-giving love. It is generous and unconditional. It is the kind of love God offers each one of us.

The Bible story for today comes from one of Paul's most famous letters. Paul is credited with writing over 25 percent of the New Testament. Paul's letters were an important part of his ministry. Whether he was in prison or just in another part of the world, Paul used his letters to communicate with other members of the early church.

The form of Paul's letters makes it obvious that he intended for them to be read aloud to the individual congregations, Through his letters Paul taught the churches. The letters begin with a salutation, continue with the reason for the letter, and close with a

benediction. He criticized the churches, corrected them, praised them, or pleaded with them, depending on what was needed at the time.

Children love letters. They enjoy writing them to friends and they especially enjoy receiving them. But the art of writing letters is fast being replaced by computer email. Children and adults are now able to reach other people around the world in just an instant. Wouldn't Paul have delighted in such a wonderful way to communicate?

In this letter Paul dwells on the qualities of love. Most children hear the word *love* and think of romantic love, but love is much more than that. Throughout the Gospels Jesus calls his disciples to love one another. Help the children see that love is more than romantic feelings. Love is the giving of self.

Love is patient and kind.

If time is limited, we recommend those activities that are noted in **boldface**. Depending on your time and the number of children, you may be able to include more activities.

ACTIVITY	TIME	SUPPLIES	
Love Squared	5 minutes	Reproducible 1A, crayons or pencils, construction paper (red, pink, white), scissors, masking tape	JOIN THE FUN
Fruit of the Spirit	**10 minutes**	**large white cloth, shallow dishes, tempera paint (red, yellow, orange, green, blue, purple), paint brushes, newspaper**	
Who Do You Love?	5 minutes	None	BIBLE STORY FUN
Great, Greater, Greatest	5 minutes	items of graduated sizes such as paper cups, paper plates, boxes; index cards or construction paper; felt-tip marker	
Bible Story: Love Is . . .	**10 minutes**	**Red felt-tip marker, long paper strips**	
Noisy Gongs	5 minutes	a variety of potentially noisy items such as metal pots, pans, lids, metal bowls, wooden spoons, empty soda cans, disposable aluminum pie pans	
Love Lights	10 minutes	Reproducible 1B; black construction paper; push pins, sharpened pencils, or wooden toothpicks; tape	
Jump, Turn, Praise!	5 minutes	None	LIVE THE FUN
Fruit Basket Prayers	**5 minutes**	**plastic fruit**	

JOIN THE FUN

Supplies

Reproducible
1A,
crayons or
pencils,
construction
paper (red,
pink, white),
scissors,
masking tape

Love Squared

Make a copy of the love square puzzle **(Reproducible 1A)** for each child.

Welcome the children as they arrive. Try to say something personal to each child. Set the stage for the discussion about love. Decorate the room with construction paper hearts. Early arrivals may help cut out hearts from the red, pink, and white construction paper and put them around the room.

Give each child a copy of the love square puzzle. Have them discover how many times the word *love* is written in the square. They can look across and down and have them circle the words with pencils or crayons. All the letters have to be together on one line. *(Love is written thirty-nine times.)*

Say: **Today's lesson is about love. Paul was a follower of Jesus. He wrote letters to his friends to tell them about living as Christians. Our Bible story is the letter Paul wrote to his friends in Corinth to tell them about love.**

> **Love is patient and kind.**

Supplies

large white
cloth, shallow
dishes,
tempera paint
(red, yellow,
orange, green,
blue, purple),
paint brushes,
newspaper

Fruit of the Spirit

The theme of the first nine lessons is called the Fruit of the Spirit. If you are teaching this as a unit and including all nine lessons, you might want to make a Fruit of the Spirit worship cloth.

Cover a work surface with newspaper. Then place the white cloth, large enough to fit the table, over the newspaper. Put shallow dishes of tempera paints around the edge.

Let the children paint simple fruit shapes onto the cloth (apples, oranges, grapes, strawberries, blueberries). Allow the cloth to dry. Place it on the altar during the worship time.

Say: **When we believe in Jesus we try to follow Jesus' example. After Jesus died, his friends continued to tell others about him. One of the things these people did was try to set an example that true believers would follow. If you believed in Jesus and were filled with the Holy Spirit, you lived a life of love, joy, peace, patience, kindness, generosity, faithfulness, gentleness, and self-control. These characteristics are called fruit of the Spirit.**

Who Do You Love?

Supplies

None

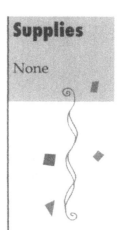

Bring the children to the center of the room.

Ask: What do you think of when you hear the word *love*? *(hugging, kissing, being in love, girlfriends and boyfriends)*

Say: Love can be all that. But love is much, much more. And in today's Bible story we will learn just what love is.

Love is patient and kind.

Say: Let's play a game about love. I will ask one of you: "Whom do you love?" Because we all love one another, the person I select will begin describing someone in the group. Don't make the clues too easy.

The rest of the group will try to decide who the person is. As soon as you think you know who the person is, go and stand behind that person. You can change your mind once. When it looks like everyone has decided, the person who is doing the describing will go and stand behind the individual she or he has chosen.

Play this game until everyone has a chance to be "loved" or until the group begins to get bored.

Great, Greater, Greatest

Supplies

items of graduated sizes such as paper cups, paper plates, boxes; index cards or construction paper; felt-tip marker

Place a variety of items that come in graduated sizes on a table or tray.

Ask: How are all these items similar? *(They all come in various sizes.)* **Find the largest in each set. The largest cup could hold the greatest amount of milk; the largest paper plate would be able to hold the greatest amount of food; the largest box would be able to hold the greatest number of items; and so forth. I have one more thing for you to think about.**

Place three index cards or pieces of construction paper on the table labeled "Faith," "Hope," and "Love."

Ask: Which of these is the greatest?

Say: We'll hear the answer in today's Bible story.

13

Love Is . . .

by Sharilyn S. Adair

> **Say:** Paul was not one of Jesus' disciples, but he became a strong leader of the Christian church. Paul traveled by land and sea to take the good news of Jesus to different cities and countries. Wherever he went Paul helped start churches. Often he wrote letters back to those churches to encourage them and to teach them more about Jesus. Paul wrote to the church at Corinth, an important city of the time, about what it takes to be a Christian. He was concerned about some of the behavior of the church members. He had heard that the Corinthian Christians were always fighting among themselves. Paul asked them to get along with one another and to treat one another with love. Listen for the word "love" as I tell what Paul wrote to these churches. Every time you hear the word, cross your arms on your chest. You will be making the American Sign Language word for *love*.

What if I could speak every language there was, even languages used by angels?

If I didn't love other people, then I would just be making a lot of noise, like a gong or a crashing cymbal.

What if I understood everything there is to know and could even predict the future?

What if I had faith strong enough to ask for a mountain to move and it did?

If I didn't love other people, I would still be nothing.

What if I gave away everything I owned and even gave up my life so people would think I was good?

If I didn't love other people I wouldn't gain anything. Those actions would be nothing to brag about.

Then what is love?
Love is patient; love is kind. Love isn't envious or jealous. Love isn't boastful or proud of being better than others.

Love is not rude. It doesn't disregard others' feelings. Love is not selfish, always wanting its own way.

14

Love does not resent others or hold grudges. Love is never cranky or irritable.

Love is in favor of the truth and doesn't like wrongdoing.

Love can bear anything that happens, always believing in others and hoping the best for them.

Love never ends. Someday everything else will end. Our languages and everything we know will be forgotten. We never can know everything, anyway; only God knows everything.

Just as adults once were children and thought and acted like children but then grew up and learned to act like adults, someday we will grow up and know God much better than we do today.

Right now we only know a part of God. It's like looking in a cloudy mirror. But one day we will see God face-to-face. Then we will know and understand God just as God knows and understands us.

Until then, we can have faith, hope, and love. And greatest of these is love.

Mobius Strip

Form a Mobius strip (about 2 to 4 inches wide) by taking a long strip of paper, twisting it once, and then gluing the ends together to form a loop.

Say: Let's draw a love line down the center of the strip and see how far it will go.

Place a red crayon or felt-tip marker anywhere on the Mobius strip and draw a line down the center of the strip.

Ask: Where will our line end?

Say: The line will go on continuously, without stopping on both sides of the paper. Look at this love line! This love never ends!

15

Noisy Gongs

Supplies

a variety of potentially noisy items such as metal pots, pans, lids, metal bowls, wooden spoons, empty soda cans, disposable aluminum pie pans

Say: First Corinthians says that even if we could speak all the languages of humans and of angels, if we did not love others, our speech would be no more than a noisy gong of a clanging cymbal.

Provide a variety of potentially "noisy" items. Invite the children to create "noisy gongs" or "clanging cymbals" with these items.

Say: I will read some words. I want you to decide if the words are loving or not. If the words are loving words, we'll all say, "Now, that's love!" But if they are not loving words, let's make loud noises with our noisemakers.

Read the words printed below. Encourage the children to respond.

**I'm the best basketball player in the entire school.
Hurry up! You're going to make me late!
Thanks for fixing dinner, Dad. I'll wash the dishes.** *(Now, that's love!)*
**Look at how much money I'm putting in the offering!
I'm sorry that I tore your picture. Please forgive me.** *(Now, that's love!)*
**You never do anything right.
You have a beautiful voice. I love to hear you sing.** *(Now, that's love!)*
**Mom always gives you the biggest piece of cake.
I won't play soccer unless I get to be the goalie.
Our math homework looks difficult. But if we help each other, I'm sure we'll be able to find the right answers.** *(Now, that's love!)*

Love Lights

Say: When we follow Jesus we can't help but love one another. This love shows all over us. It shines like a light from inside of us.

> ## Love is patient and kind.

Give each child a copy of the love lights picture **(Reproducible 1B)**. Tape the picture to a sheet of black construction paper so that it will not slip as the children are punching out the design.

Let children punch out the design using the push pins, sharpened pencils, or toothpicks. Caution them not to miss a single dot. When the children are finished, let them hold the picture up to the window or a light. The design will shine through the holes.

Jump, Turn, Praise!

Supplies

None

Sing the song "Fruit of the Spirit Jump" to the tune of "Pick a Bale of Cotton." Encourage the children to do the motions as they sing together.

Fruit of the Spirit Jump

Gonna jump down, turn around
(Jump; turn around.)
Show my love and praise God.
(Cross arms over chest; raise arms.)
Jump down, turn around,
(Jump; turn around.)
Show my love and praise!
(Cross arms over chest; raise arms.)

Gonna jump down, turn around
(Jump; turn around.)
Stomp my feet and praise God.
(Stomp feet; raise arms.)
Jump down, turn around,
(Jump; turn around.)
Stomp my feet and praise!
(Stomp feet; raise arms.)

Gonna jump down, turn around
(Jump; turn around.)
Clap my hands and praise God.
(Stomp feet; raise arms.)
Jump down, turn around,
(Jump; turn around.)
Clap my hands and praise!
(Stomp feet; raise arms.)

Gonna jump down, turn around
(Jump; turn around.)
Swing my hips and praise God.
(Swing hips; raise arms.)
Jump down, turn around,
(Jump; turn around.)
Swing my hips and praise!
(Swing hips; raise arms.)

© 2001 Abingdon Press

Fruit Basket Prayers

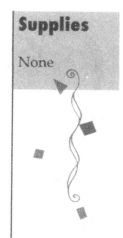

Supplies

plastic fruit

Have the children stand in a circle. Hold a piece of plastic fruit.

Say: Love is one of the fruit of the Spirit. Paul wrote a letter to tell his friends about love. Our Bible verse is from Paul's letter: "Love is patient; love is kind" (1 Corinthians 13:4).

Toss the plastic fruit to one of the children in the circle.

Pray: Dear God, we thank you for *(child's name)*. Help *(him or her)* show love to others by being patient and kind. Amen.

Then have the child toss the plastic fruit to another child. Pray for that child. Continue tossing the fruit around the circle until everyone has had a turn.

Love is patient and kind.

How many times can you find the word *love* in the square?

```
L O V E L O V E L O V
O V E L O V E L O V E
V E L O V E L O V E L
E L O V E L O V E L O
L O V E L O V E L O V
O V E L O V E L O V E
V E L O V E L O V E L
E L O V E L O V E L O
L O V E L O V E L O V
O V E L O V E L O V E
```

Love is patient; love is kind.
1 Corinthians 13:4

Let your love light shine!

Joy

Bible Verse

Sing for joy to the LORD, all the earth.

Psalm 98:4, GNT

Bible Story

Galatians 5:22–23; Matthew 28:1–10; Mark 16:1–8;
Luke 24:1–12; John 20:1–18

JESUS LIVES! The hope of Christianity is centered on this joyous event. The disciples struggled with what was happening and why it happened the way it did in the Gospel accounts of the arrest, trial, and execution of Jesus. They saw their great hopes for Jesus vanish in the events of these tumultuous twenty-four hours. They were now afraid and filled with sorrow.

Mary Magdalene and the other Mary went to Jesus' tomb in Matthew's Gospel account of the Resurrection. The men did not go with them. Upon arriving at the tomb they found an angel of the Lord, who told them that they would not find Jesus in the tomb. He had been raised from the dead! This angel then told the women to go and tell the news to the disciples.

The women were running "with fear and great joy" to tell the disciples what had happened when they met Jesus himself!

When something this exciting and this joyful happens it is impossible not to tell everyone you meet!

But the fact that Jesus lives means more than exciting news. Jesus' resurrection assures us that God does triumph over all. It shows us that sinful separation from God and death is not all there is for us, but that God brings life out of death! Hope lives and that hope is for us. This joyful resurrection experience shapes our lives in powerful new ways—ways that we will want to tell others about. All of this is such good news!

Children experience joy. Just watch the exuberance with which they greet an exciting experience or an unexpected opportunity. Help them relate this joy to an even greater sense of joy that they will grow into as Christians.

We are filled with joy because Jesus lives!

If time is limited, we recommend those activities that are noted in **boldface**. Depending on your time and the number of children, you may be able to include more activities.

ACTIVITY	TIME	SUPPLIES	
Extra! Good News!	**10 minutes**	**Reproducible 2A; pencils, crayons, or felt-tip markers**	JOIN THE FUN
Sculptor and Clay	5 minutes	None	
Jump, Turn, Praise!	5 minutes	None	BIBLE STORY FUN
All for One	10 minutes	None	
Bible Story: Sing for Joy!	**10 minutes**	**None**	
High Five Hand Jive	10 minutes	None	
Jars of Bible Joy	10 minutes	Reproducible 2B, scissors, glass jars, pinking shears, fabric scraps, white glue, small paper bowls, newspaper, old paintbrushes, neon acrylic poster paints, rubber bands	LIVE THE FUN
Fruit Basket Prayers	**5 minutes**	**plastic fruit**	

Supplies

Reproducible 2A; pencils, crayons, or felt-tip markers

Extra! Good News!

Make a copy of the Good News Gazette! **(Reproducible 2A)** for each child or each pair of children.

Ask: What if there were only good news allowed in your daily newspaper? What would happen if there were no murders? no one stole anything? nothing bad happened to anyone? What would a newspaper look like?

Say: Here's your chance to make a nothing-but-good-news newspaper. Today, we are going to learn about joy, one of the fruit of the Spirit. Who do you think had joy? *(The children will probably say shepherds and talk about the birth of Jesus. But tell them that the good news was even greater than that.)*

> ## We are filled with joy because Jesus lives!

Encourage the children to write and draw good news stories on the Good News Gazette. Help the children think of good news stories like "Tomb Found Empty!" or "Angels Sighted in Jerusalem." Photocopy the finished newspaper and let the children distribute it to church members.

Supplies

None

Sculptor and Clay

Divide the children into pairs.

Say: I want you to create a statue. One of you will be the sculptor; the other will be the clay. The sculptor will create a statue from the clay. The statue will be called "JOY." The only catch is that the sculptor may not touch the clay in any way. The sculptor may only use words.

Let the partners decide who will be the sculptor and who will be the clay. Words the sculpture might use are: "Bend at the wrist," or "Stretch your arm toward the ceiling," or "Open your mouth."

When the masterpiece is completed, the sculptor will show his or her work to the rest of the class or group. Then the partners will reverse roles and the artistic process will begin again.

Say: Today we are learning about joy, one of the fruit of the Spirit.

Jump, Turn, Praise!

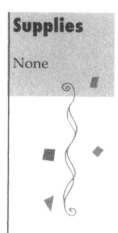

Sing the song "Fruit of the Spirit Jump" to the tune of "Pick a Bale of Cotton." Encourage the children to do the motions as they sing together.

Fruit of the Spirit Jump

Gonna jump down, turn around
(Jump; turn around.)
Show my joy and praise God.
(Pat hands on chest many times; raise arms.)
Jump down, turn around,
(Jump; turn around.)
Show my joy and praise!
(Pat hands on chest many times; raise arms.)

Gonna jump down, turn around
(Jump; turn around.)
Show my love and praise God.
(Cross arms over chest; raise arms.)
Jump down, turn around,
(Jump; turn around.)
Show my love and praise!
(Cross arms over chest; raise arms.)

Gonna jump down, turn around
(Jump; turn around.)
Stomp my feet and praise God.
(Stomp feet; raise arms.)
Jump down, turn around,
(Jump; turn around.)
Stomp my feet and praise!
(Stomp feet; raise arms.)

Gonna jump down, turn around
(Jump; turn around.)
Swing my hips and praise God.
(Swing hips; raise arms.)
Jump down, turn around,
(Jump; turn around.)
Swing my hips and praise!
(Swing hips; raise arms.)

© 2001 Abingdon Press

All for One!

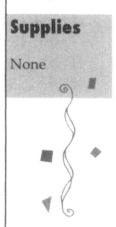

Have the children form at least two groups. Let each group select a town crier. The town crier is responsible for shouting "Oh, joy!" for the group.

Say: Our Bible story today is about a very joyful event. Everybody likes to be joyful and happy. But not everyone agrees upon just what makes them happy. Everyone in your group in this game must agree on one thing that makes all of you happy. For example, I'll ask: "What makes you happy at school?" Your group must find an answer you all agree on. If even one person doesn't agree, you must find another answer. As soon as your team agrees, then the town crier will shout "Oh, joy!"

Use the following situations for the children to try to agree upon:
What makes you happy in the summer?   on your birthday?
What makes you happy in the morning?   in the evening?
What makes you happy at church?   at home?

Say: It's not always easy to agree on everything. But the following story tells about one thing that everyone can agree on!

23

Sing for Joy

by LeeDell Stickler

> **Say: We know the story of Jesus, how he was born in a stable and welcomed by angels. We've heard about the wise men and the day he stayed behind at the Temple. We know that Jesus taught his followers to love one another, to be kind, and to care for others. Today we talk about the most joy-filled day, the day God raised Jesus from the dead.**
>
> *Invite the children to participate in telling the story as you demonstrate certain actions after each stanza of the story-poem.*

It happened on a Sunday
Just as the sun began to rise
A quiet filled the garden
As the daylight touched the sky.
(Lie down and pretend to be asleep.)

Tip-tap went the footsteps
Upon the cobbled streets.
But it was much too early
For friends to meet or greet.
(Tiptoe in place.)

Two women walked so sadly
Toward the garden's gate
For they were on a mission.
One that could not wait.
(Walk sadly.)

They came to say a last goodbye,
To their teacher and their friend.
For on a cross of splintered wood
His life came to an end.
(Pretend to cry.)

They'd put him in a borrowed tomb
With the sabbath fast approaching.
No time to say some final words,
With all those folks encroaching.
(Shrink back in fear.)

But sabbath now had come and gone
'Twas time to do their duty.
They came to the garden on the hill,
A place of quiet beauty.
(Tiptoe and put finger to lips.)

What will we do, the women thought
There's a stone across the door—
Even though it's round in shape,
Moving it's too big a chore.
(Put finger tip to forehead.)

But as they neared the garden tomb
Strange things began to happen.
The guards that had been posted there
Now looked like they were nappin'.
(Put hand to forehead.)

ALL-IN-ONE BIBLE FUN

The ground began to tremble,
And the trees began to sway.
As an angel from the realm of God
Just rolled the stone away.
(Put hands over mouth in fear.)

The angel looked like lightning,
His clothes were white as snow.
He scared the women half to death
And so they turned to go.
(Turn away.)

"Don't be afraid," the angel said.
"For Jesus is not here.
God has raised him, as he'd said,
There is no need to fear."
(Raise arms up toward sky.)

"Come and look inside the tomb
And see where Jesus lay.
Then go quickly to his friends
And this is what you'll say."
(Shake finger.)

"We know that Jesus isn't dead.
We know he lives today.
You'll find him now in Galilee,
So you must be on your way."
(Point to the distance.)

The Marys left the garden then,
To the town they ran with haste.
The greatest news of all, they knew
And not a moment could they waste.
(Run in place.)

Then suddenly upon the road
They saw him standing there.
"Peace to you," he said to them
As they both came near.
(Stop suddenly and throw up hands.)

At first the Marys were afraid
They fell straight to the ground.
They reached right out to touch him,
"Was he really safe and sound?"
(Fall to ground.)

And his feet they felt with both
their hands
Were feet just like their own.
They felt just like the normal kind
With skin, and hair, and bone.
(Reach out hands as though touching feet.)

Jesus reached right down and said,
"There's no time for fuss and
bother.
You must go and tell my friends,
And they must tell the others."
(Walk in place.)

And according to the Bible,
They did just what he said.
And all the ones who doubted
Learned that Jesus wasn't dead.
(Hold hands in front like a book.)

We know that Jesus lives again.
We've heard the Bible story.
Our hearts are filled with love and joy,
To God we give the glory.
(Hold hands up toward sky and wave.)

Supplies

None

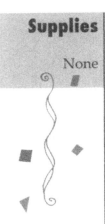

High Five Hand Jive

Have the children form a large circle. Make sure there is space to move without running into anything. The children will stand facing the center with their hands behind them, palms up.

Say: When Mary came to the tomb that morning, she got a big surprise. She came in sadness, ready to prepare Jesus' body for burial. But instead, she found an angel who told her that Jesus was alive. Then she came face-to-face with Jesus himself. What happiness! What joy! Mary couldn't keep the news to herself—she had to hurry to tell the others. So she ran all the way. We too, as followers of Jesus, can share the joy of Jesus' resurrection with others.

Continue: Let's play a game. I want you to pretend that you are all Jesus' disciples. I will select one of you to be the one who found the empty tomb. That person will walk around the outside of the circle and slap the hands of one of the disciples. The two of you will then run in opposite directions, racing for the vacant spot. Upon meeting at the other side of the circle, stop, and the first person will say,"Jesus is alive!" and the other person will respond, "Hallelujah!" Then you will both give a High Five Hand Jive.

The High Five Hand Jive is done as follows:
1. Hit right hands together.
2. Hit left hands together.
3. Hit both hands together.
4. First player holds hands in front of body palms up and second player slaps them.
5. Second player holds hands in front of body with palms up and first player hits them.
6. Bump right hips twice.
7. Bump left hips twice.

Continue: When this ritual is complete, then both players will continue around the circle, racing for the vacant place. The first one there will get to keep the place. The second person will become "IT" and begin walking around the circle. Players will be eliminated who fail to stop and say "Jesus is risen!" and "Hallelujah!" and do the High Five Hand Jive.

We are filled with joy because Jesus lives!

Jars of Bible Joy

Make a copy of the letters and Bible verses **(Reproducible 2B)** for each child. Give each child a clean glass jar. Cover the work surface with newspaper.

Reproducible 2B, scissors, glass jars, pinking shears, fabric scraps, white glue, small paper bowls, newspaper, old paint-brushes, neon acrylic poster paints, rubber bands

Say: When we follow Jesus we can't help but feel the joy of knowing that Jesus lives. The Bible is filled with verses that reassure us and fill us with joy. We are going to make Jars of Bible Joy to keep in our rooms. We can reach into our jars whenever we are feeling down, and pull out a joyful Bible verse that will remind us that we are special to God.

Pour small amounts of white glue into paper bowls. Tint the glue by adding small amounts of neon acrylic poster paint to each bowl. Have the children cut out the letters and the verses. First paint the jar with the colored glues. Then place the letters on the jar. Paint over them with the glue.

Cut a fabric circle about one inch larger than the lid of the jar. Put glue on the jar lid. Center the lid on the fabric circle. Put a rubber band around the rim, holding the fabric until it dries.

Place the Bible verses in the jars. Set the jars aside to dry. (A hair dryer will speed up the process if the children want to take the jars home.)

Fruit Basket Prayers

Have the children stand in a circle. Hold a piece of plastic fruit.

Supplies

plastic fruit

Say: Joy is one of the fruit of the Spirit. Our Bible verse is "Sing for joy to the LORD, all the earth" (Psalm 98:4, GNT). As Christians we are filled with joy because we know Jesus is alive.

Toss the plastic fruit to one of the children in the circle.

Pray: Dear God, we thank you for *(child's name).* **Help** *(him or her)* **be filled with joy because we know Jesus is alive. Amen.**

Then have the child toss the plastic fruit to another child. Pray for that child. Continue tossing the fruit around the circle until everyone has had a turn.

We are filled with joy because Jesus lives!

Good News Gazette!

A Good News Newspaper   *Vol. 1*

REPRODUCIBLE 2A

J O Y

Nothing in all creation will be able to separate us from the love of God in Christ Jesus our Lord. Romans 8:39, adapted	Remember, I will be with you and protect you wherever you go. Genesis 28:15, GNT	Shout for joy for what the LORD has done. Psalm 33:1, GNT	For God so loved the world that he gave his one Son, so that everyone who believes in him may not perish but may have eternal life. John 3:16	And remember, I am with you always, to the end of the age. Matthew 28:20

Peace

Bible Verse

Blessed are the peacemakers, for they will be called children of God.

Matthew 5:9

Bible Story

Galatians 5:22–23; 1 Samuel 25:1–35

This story of David occurs during the time before he is king. David and his men, having escaped the palace of King Saul, are roaming the countrysides. This made the procurement of enough food to feed the group a problem. At the time of the sheep-shearing festival David and his men had been camped near the place where Nabal's flocks were grazing. They had protected Nabal's valuable flocks from thieves by camping there. So when supplies began to run short, David requested that Nabal give David and his men food and drink in exchange for this help.

Nabal treated David's men with disrespect and turned them away—a major breach of Middle Eastern hospitality. David was angry, and decided to respond to this insult by attacking and destroying Nabal.

One of Nabal's shepherds went to Abigail, Nabal's wife. Abigail at once realized that her husband's rash response had put them in grave danger. Nabal's actions were an insult, even though David's reaction was impetuous. Abigail saw that something must be done—and quickly.

Abigail deliberately chose peace. She brought to David and his men more provisions than were requested. She then bowed humbly before David and asked forgiveness for her husband's foolishness. Abigail kept peace not only for her family, but also for David and his men. She showed that disputes can be settled peacefully when people are generous—and do not always have to be right in the eyes of others.

Sometimes children must compromise. This doesn't mean giving up all their beliefs—it just means that once in a while peacemaking is more important than winning. Help the children learn the difference.

We can be peacemakers.

If time is limited, we recommend those activities that are noted in **boldface**. Depending on your time and the number of children, you may be able to include more activities.

Activity	Time	Supplies	
What Is It?	**5 minutes**	**Reproducible 3A; pencils, crayons, or felt-tip markers**	JOIN THE FUN
Mission Impossible	10 minutes	paper plates; red, blue, and green felt-tip markers; plastic coins, crayons, or paper clips	
Jump, Turn, Praise!	5 minutes	None	BIBLE STORY FUN
Push Me, Pull You	10 minutes	None	
Bible Story: Showdown at the Baa Baa Corral	**10 minutes**	**Optional: cowboy hats, bandannas, apron, ropes, fake moustache, western gear**	
Peace and Love	15 minutes	Reproducible 3B, scissors, lightweight cardboard, construction paper (red, white, pink, purple), white paper plates, red yarn, white glue, tape, paper punch	
Children of God	5 minutes	None	LIVE THE FUN
Fruit Basket Prayers	**5 minutes**	**plastic fruit**	

31

Supplies

Reproducible 3A; pencils, crayons or felt-tip markers

What Is It?

Make a copy of the dot-to-dot puzzle (**Reproducible 3A**) for each child in the group.

Welcome the children as they come into the room. Try to say something personal to each child. Remind them that they are all children of God. Have the children connect the dots with pencils, crayons, or felt-tip makers to discover an animal.

Say: Today the fruit of the Spirit is peace. This puzzle shows an animal that we have come to think of when we talk about peace.

> We can be peacemakers.

Mission Impossible

Supplies

paper plates; red, blue, and green felt-tip markers; plastic coins, crayons, or paper clips

Divide the children into two teams—the red team and the blue team. On one paper plate draw a red happy face. On a second plate draw a blue happy face. On a third draw a green happy face. Place all the coins on the plate with the green happy face. If you don't have plastic coins, use something from the room such as crayons or paperclips. Place the two other paper plates in opposite corners of the room.

Say: Each team has a special mission. I will have to whisper it to you.

Tell the red team that their mission is to move one coin at a time from the green or blue happy face to the red happy face. When all of the coins are on the red happy face the game is over. Then tell the blue team that their mission is to move the coins one at a time from the green or red happy face to the blue happy face. The game is over when all of the coins are on the blue happy face.

Say: When I say "Go!", then the game begins. Remember—you may only carry one coin at a time. You have five minutes to complete your mission.

Have the children stop after a few minutes and come to sit on the floor.

Ask: What happened? *(They had conflicting missions.)* **Was this an impossible mission?** *(yes)* **What would have been an easier solution?**

Say: Today's Bible story is about peace and conflict and being peacemakers. *(Read the Bible verse.)*

Jump, Turn, Praise!

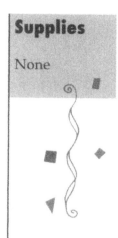

Sing the song "Fruit of the Spirit Jump" to the tune of "Pick a Bale of Cotton." Encourage the children to do the motions as they sing together.

Fruit of the Spirit Jump

Gonna jump down, turn around
(Jump; turn around.)
Show my peace and praise God.
(Make a peace sign; raise arms.)
Jump down, turn around,
(Jump; turn around.)
Show my peace and praise!
(Make a peace sign; raise arms.)

Gonna jump down, turn around
(Jump; turn around.)
Show my love and praise God.
(Cross arms over chest; raise arms.)
Jump down, turn around,
(Jump; turn around.)
Show my love and praise!
(Cross arms over chest; raise arms.)

Gonna jump down, turn around
(Jump; turn around.)
Show my joy and praise God.
(Pat hands on chest many times; raise arms.)
Jump down, turn around,
(Jump; turn around.)
Show my joy and praise!
(Pat hands on chest many times; raise arms.)

Gonna jump down, turn around
(Jump; turn around)
Swing my hips and praise God.
(Swing hips; raise arms.)
Jump down, turn around,
(Jump; turn around.)
Swing my hips and praise!
(Swing hips; raise arms.)

Push Me, Pull You

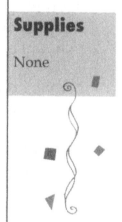

Divide the children into partners. Each partner will try to push the other partner's hands (or fake it by changing the force of push, backing hands off, and so forth) from this position until one of the players is forced to move one or both feet. Collect points. If a partner moves then the other partner gets the point. The first partner to collect five points is the winner.

Ask: What determines who wins this game? *(whoever is stronger, or pushes harder, or is sneakier)* **What would happen if neither of you ever pushed?** *(there wouldn't be a winner)* **Would there be a loser?** *(no)*

Have the children hold their hands in position and not push. No one will be forced to move or to step aside.

Say: Today's Bible story is about someone who worked to keep the peace. It didn't make any difference to her what was right or wrong, or who was right or wrong—the important thing was that the two groups of people avoid fighting. This woman's name was Abigail, and she was a peacemaker.

Showdown at the Baa Baa Corral

by LeeDell Stickler

> *Today's Bible story is written in the form of a western. You will need a narrator and these characters: Nabal, the wealthy but insensitive sheep rancher; Miss Abigail, his beautiful and peace-loving wife; Marshal David, the handsome young peace officer; Lefty, the ranch hand; and Shorty, the chuckwagon cook. If you have cowboy hats and bandannas, let the children wear these. Nabal might wear a moustache. Shorty could wear an apron and Lefty might carry a rope.*

Narrator: Gather 'round, folks, I've gotta story to tell you about a no-good skinflint named Nabal, his pretty wife Miss Abigail, and a handsome young marshal named Marshal David. Now, the story begins about sheep-shearing time at the Baa Baa Ranch. Nabal had a passel of sheep and was very rich. But he was also stingy.

Nabal: I didn't get rich by giving my money away. What's mine is mine.

Narrator: Nabal had a beautiful wife whose name was Miss Abigail. She was a good-hearted woman who always tried to do what was right.

Miss Abigail: Howdy, ya'll.

Narrator: It seems Marshall David and his posse came riding through the territory. They set up camp near Nabal's ranch, keeping a watch for any sheep rustlers who might be working the area.

David: *(sweeps off hat and bows)* Howdy, folks. Proud to meet ya.

Narrator: Now as Shorty the chuckwagon cook was taking stock of supplies, he saw that they were running a bit short.

Shorty: Marshal David, we're running a bit short on grub.

Marshal David: Shorty, take the chuckwagon over to that spread we passed yesterday. Ask the rancher if we could have some grub just to tide us over a spell. We've been protecting his sheep from sheep rustlers, after all.

Narrator: So Shorty headed to the Baa Baa Ranch.

Lefty: Stop right where you are. Put your hands in the air and walk forward slowly.

Shorty: *(Walks up to Nabal in a bow-legged fashion.)* Don't shoot. I've come for Marshal David and his posse. We've run out of food and are powerful hungry. Could you spare us some grub?

Nabal: Git your dirty boots offa my land, you lazy, good-for-nothing cowpoke. I don't know Marshal David and I don't like your face. Now git, before I put a cactus in yore britches.

Narrator: Shorty got into the wagon and high-tailed it back to camp.

Marshal David: Where's the grub?

Shorty: Well, Marshal, you aren't gonna like this. That snake ran me off his spread and even threatened to put cactus in my drawers.

Marshal David: Now, that isn't very friendly. Mount up, boys. It's time for a showdown at the Baa Baa corral.

Narrator: Meanwhile, back at the ranch.

Lefty: Miss Abigail, may I have a word?

Miss Abigail: Sure, Lefty.

Lefty: I know you are a good woman who always wants to do what's right. Your worthless husband has just gotten us into a passel of trouble.

Miss Abigail: *(Sighs.)* What did he do this time?

Lefty: Marshal David and his posse came a-lookin' for food. Your skinflint husband refused to give them any food and sent them away. That isn't right, Miss Abigail. We're supposed to share with travelers. I wouldn't be surprised if we don't see a shootin' match about sundown.

Miss Abigail: Hitch up the wagon, Lefty, and load it down with grub. I'm gonna make a run to the canyon and see if I can stop a range war.

Narrator: Miss Abigail loaded up the wagon and high-tailed it into the canyon. She met Marshal David and his posse coming 'round the bend. They were itching for a fight.

Miss Abigail: Whoa, there! Oh, Marshal David, turn back. You don't want to do what you're planning! My husband has no manners. But just see what I've brought you. It's even more than you asked for!

Marshall David: Why, thank you, Miss Abigail. God must have sent you here to keep me from making a powerful mistake.

Narrator: David accepted the food and Miss Abigail returned to the ranch. There was no showdown at the Baa Baa corral. Miss Abigail had kept the peace.

Supplies

Reproducible 3B, light-weight cardboard, scissors, construction paper (red, white, pink, purple), white paper plates, red yarn, white glue, tape, paper punch

Peace and Love

Make a copy of the dove and heart patterns **(Reproducible 3B)** for each child.

Except for the heart with the Bible verse, trace the patterns onto lightweight cardboard (such as old file folders). Then use the patterns to cut multiple doves and hearts for the project. You will need approximately four to six doves and ten hearts in a variety of sizes. If the children have a certain dexterity with scissors, they may cut their own hearts and not use the patterns.

Say: In today's Bible story we met a young woman named Abigail. In Bible times women were not considered men's equals. They were, in fact, mostly thought of as property. But in today's story Abigail solved a problem early, before it could become a much bigger problem. She stepped in and kept one person from doing something he would have regretted. Abigail did not cause the problem; however, she stepped in to find the solution to the problem. Sometimes we are called to step in to be peacemakers. We may not have caused the problem, but we can sometimes help people stop the conflict.

Have each of the children cut out the centers of white paper plates, leaving the outside rims of the plates.

Using the patterns, cut out doves and hearts. Then using the diagram as a guide, let children glue the doves and hearts around the outsides of the plates.

When the rims of the plates are entirely covered the children may cut out hearts the same size as the Bible verse heart.

Glue that heart onto a construction paper heart. Punch a hole in the tops of the hearts and thread a length of yarn through the holes. Adjust so that the hearts hang down in the centers of the plates. Then attach another piece of yarn to make a hanger for each of the plates.

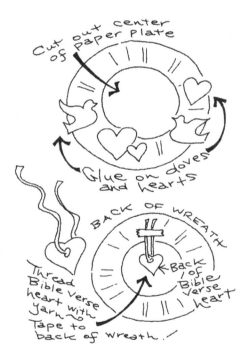

We can be peacemakers.

Children of God

Say: Today we learned about another fruit of the Spirit—peace. When the Holy Spirit lives in us, we feel at peace and we want others to feel at peace, too. So we work for peace. We become peacemakers when we work for peace.

Read the Bible verse from the Bible.

Ask: But how can we be peacemakers? What can you as boys and girls do to be peacemakers? *(Let the children make responses.)* What happens when you are a peacemaker? *(I am a child of God.)*

Teach the children signs from American Sign Language for "I am a child of God." Then let them repeat what they have suggested and respond with the signing— "When I stop my friends from arguing, then 'I am a child of God,'" or "When I play fair, then 'I am a child of God,'" for example.

Supplies

None

Fruit Basket Prayers

Have the children stand in a circle. Hold a piece of plastic fruit.

Say: Peace is one of the fruit of the Spirit. Our Bible verse is "Blessed are the peacemakers, for they will be called children of God" (Matthew 5:9). As Christians we work for peace.

Toss the plastic fruit to one of the children in the circle.

Pray: Dear God, we thank you for your child, *(child's name)*. Help *(him or her)* be a peacemaker. Amen.

Then have the child toss the plastic fruit to another child. Pray for that child. Continue tossing the fruit around the circle until everyone has had a turn.

Supplies

plastic fruit

> We can be peacemakers.

Fruit of the Spirit - Elementary

What Is It?

This animal is a symbol of peace and the Holy Spirit.

ALL-IN-ONE BIBLE FUN

Blessed are the peacemakers, for they will be called children of God. (Matthew 5:9)

Cut out center of paper plate

Glue on doves and hearts

BACK OF WREATH

Back of Bible verse heart

Thread Bible verse heart with yarn. Tape to back of wreath.

All-in-One
BIBLE ELEMENTARY
FUN

Patience

Bible Verse

Be patient and wait for the LORD to act.

Psalm 37:7, GNT

Bible Story

Galatians 5:22–23; Genesis 12:1–9; 15:1–20; 17:1–22; 18:1–15; 21:1–7

If anyone ever needed patience it was Abraham and Sarah. Twenty-five years had passed since God first promised to make of Abram a great nation. Now God was speaking again. Abram's and Sarai's names were changed to Abraham and Sarah as a symbol of God's covenant with them. God's covenant was an everlasting covenant to be the God of a great people descended from Abraham and Sarah. Abraham—at the ripe old age of ninety-nine—had a good laugh at this. This didn't seem like a likely possibility.

Sarah was having doubts that God was going to come through with that all-important child. After all, how can one have descendants without having children and time had by all human standards, already run out for her childbearing years.

Hospitality in Bible times was more than a courtesy; it was a duty. Since Abraham and Sarah lived in the desert, visitors who were turned away might die of starvation or thirst. When the three strangers came to Abraham's and Sarah's tent, Abraham greeted them and wound up entertaining God. The promise that Sarah would bear a son was given again. This time it was Sarah who laughed.

But God's promise was finally fulfilled and a son was born to Abraham and Sarah. He was named Isaac, whose name means "laughter." Sarah rejoiced, "God has brought laughter for me; everyone who hears will laugh with me."

Patience is not a virtue that elementary children possess in great abundance. Help them understand that persons had to wait for God to act throughout the Bible. During this time of waiting persons almost always learned important lessons that affected them mightily. Think of the number of years persons had to wait for the coming Savior.

We can be patient and trust in God.

If time is limited, we recommend those activities that are noted in **boldface**. Depending on your time and the number of children, you may be able to include more activities.

ACTIVITY	TIME	SUPPLIES	
Star-Studded Promise	**5 minutes**	**Reproducible 4A, pencils, construction paper, scissors, paper punch, yarn or string**	JOIN THE FUN
Dippety Dip	10 minutes	belts, yarn or string, coffee cans or shortening cans (one can for every two children), colored construction paper, masking tape, plastic toy figures	
Jump, Turn, Praise!	5 minutes	None	BIBLE STORY FUN
The Laughing Game	10 minutes	None	
Bible Story: Wait for the Lord	**10 minutes**	**None**	
Gazillions of Grains	5 minutes	table salt or sand, black construction paper, small clear glass bottle, wooden toothpicks	
Surprise! Surprise!	10 minutes	Reproducible 4B, scissors	
Bible Verse Sit-in	10 minutes	index cards, felt-tip marker	LIVE THE FUN
Fruit Basket Prayers	**5 minutes**	**plastic fruit**	

JOIN THE FUN

Star-Studded Promise

Make a copy of the star code message **(Reproducible 4A)** for each child. Decorate the room with stars cut from construction paper. Let the stars hang from the ceiling in great volume, if possible. Let early arrivals help you make stars and hang them (it will take about 10 to 15 minutes) or you can cut and hang them beforehand.

Welcome the children as they arrive. Hospitality is a duty of the church. Make sure each child feels a part of this group.

Say: **Today's Bible story is about two people who received a promise from God. You will decode this promise in the puzzle. Remember, the hardest part was waiting for the promise. The two people in this story were not young; in fact, they were quite old. They were afraid they would wait and wait and soon it would be too late. But they underestimated God. These two people had to learn to be patient. Patience is a fruit of the Spirit.**

> ## We can be patient and trust in God.

Supplies

belts, yarn or string, coffee cans or shortening cans (one can for every two children), colored construction paper, masking tape, plastic toy figures

Dippety Dip

Divide the children into teams of two players. Assign each team a can. Cover each can in a different color construction paper. Use masking tape to indicate the starting line. Place the covered cans on the opposite side of the room.

Have the partners decide who is going to do the Dippety Dip first. The other partner will be the spotter. The Dippety belt is made by tying a string to the back of a belt. At the end of the string tie a plastic toy figure. The figure should hang down in the back of the player about twelve inches from the floor.

Say: **When I say "go," each person wearing the belt will run to her or his can and try to place the figure in the can by squatting down. As soon as the figure goes into the can, the spotter yells "Dippety Dip!" and the team gets a point. Then the person with the belt rushes back to the line, where each person gives his or her partner the belt, and the game begins again. The team wins that has the most points in three minutes.**

When the three minutes are up, bring the children to the open space.

Ask: **What strategy did you learn from this game?** *(You couldn't rush. You had to be patient and take your time.)*

42

Jump, Turn, Praise!

Supplies

None

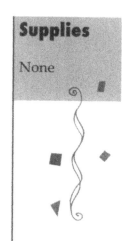

Sing the song "Fruit of the Spirit Jump" to the tune of "Pick a Bale of Cotton." Encourage the children to do the motions as they sing together.

Fruit of the Spirit Jump

Gonna jump down, turn around
(Jump; turn around.)
Be patient and praise God.
(Tap toes; raise arms.)
Jump down, turn around,
(Jump; turn around.)
Be patient and praise!
(Tap toes; raise arms.)

Gonna jump down, turn around
(Jump; turn around.)
Show my peace and praise God.
(Make a peace sign; raise arms.)
Jump down, turn around,
(Jump; turn around.)
Show my peace and praise!
(Make a peace sign; raise arms.)

Gonna jump down, turn around
(Jump; turn around.)
Show my joy and praise God.
(Pat hands on chest many times; raise arms.)
Jump down, turn around,
(Jump; turn around)
Show my joy and praise!
(Pat hands on chest many times; raise arms.)

Gonna jump down, turn around
(Jump; turn around.)
Show my love and praise God.
(Cross arms over chest; raise arms.)
Jump down, turn around,
(Jump; turn around.)
Show my love and praise!
(Cross arms over chest; raise arms.)

© 2001 Abingdon Press

The Laughing Game

Supplies

None

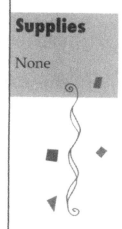

Have the children sit in a circle in chairs or on the floor. Join the group.

Say: We're going to play a laughing game. But the object of the game is to not laugh. I will start the non-laughing laughing game. I will turn to the person on my right *(say that person's name)* **and say "ha." That person will then turn to the person on his or her right and say "ha, ha." That person will then turn to the next person to the right and say "ha, ha, ha." We will continue adding a "ha" until we get all the way around the circle. Persons who are passing the laugh must look directly into the eyes of the person they are speaking to as the word "ha" is passed. Remember, don't laugh or we have to start all over again.**

Keep reminding the children not to laugh. After two or three attempts to get around the circle, stop the game.

Say: It's fun to laugh. Let's listen to the story today and find out who laughed and why.

Wait for the Lord

by LeeDell Stickler

Teach the children the signs for American Sign Language.

Be—*hold palm forward, thumb down; place a fist with the thumb on the outside against the lips and draw downward;*
wait—*hold left hand, palm up, a little away from the left side; then hold right hand in the same position nearer the body with the fingers pointing toward the left wrist; wiggle the fingers;*
for—*with index finger point toward the right side of the forehead, circle downward and forward, ending with the index finger pointing forward at eye level;*
Lord—*place the right "L" at the left shoulder, then on the right waist.*

Practice the movements so that the children are familiar with them.

Say: Today whenever you hear the phrase, "and they waited for God to keep the promise," everyone will stand up and sign the verse.

A long time ago there lived a man named Abraham and his wife, Sarah. They were happy except that they didn't have any children.

One day God spoke to Abraham. "I want you to go to a land that I will show you. If you do this, I will give you many children and grandchildren."

Now Abraham and Sarah were very old—much too old to be having children—but Abraham and Sarah trusted God. So, they packed up all their belongings and set off to the new land that God would show them. And they waited for God to keep the promise. *(Sign the verse.)*

Time passed. Abraham and Sarah were not getting any younger. One day Abraham and Sarah came to a beautiful land. God told them, "One day, all this land will belong to your children and to their children." Abraham and Sarah knew that they were very old. They also knew that they didn't have any children—yet. But they trusted God and they waited for God to keep the promise. *(Sign the verse.)*

God cared for Abraham and Sarah as they traveled. Their flocks of sheep and goats grew larger. Life

ALL-IN-ONE BIBLE FUN

was very good for them. God continued to move them from place to place. They trusted God and they waited for God to keep the promise. *(Sign the verse.)*

Finally Abraham and Sarah came to the land that God had promised them. It was a beautiful land, with food for them and for their animals. Once again God told them, "All the land that you see, I will give to you and to your children forever. And your children will be as many as the dust of the earth or the stars in the sky."

Abraham looked at Sarah. Sarah looked at Abraham. Neither would say what they were thinking. They were old, much too old to be thinking of having children. But still they trusted God and they waited for God to keep the promise. *(Sign the verse.)*

One day as Abraham was resting in the shade of the tent, three strangers came walking. Visitors did not usually come into this part of the wilderness. So Abraham rushed to greet them.

"Welcome," Abraham said. "Will you stop for awhile? Rest under the shade of our tree. I will bring you food to eat and cool water to drink." Abraham called for his servants. Abraham and Sarah were happy to share what they had because there was so little food in the wilderness and visitors were always welcomed.

As the strangers finished their meal, one of the men said to Abraham, "When we come this way next year, you and your wife will have a baby boy."

Sarah overheard what the man said. She began to giggle. Then she snickered. Then she chuckled. Finally she laughed out loud. God had promised her a child. But she was over ninety years old!

The stranger looked over at the tent. "Why is Sarah laughing? Doesn't she know that with God anything is possible?"

When the next year came, Abraham and Sarah had a beautiful son. Sarah named him "Isaac," whose name means "laughter." Sarah remembered how she had laughed when the stranger had told her about his birth. Every time Abraham and Sarah looked at their baby, they remembered God's promise and remembered to *(Sign the Bible verse.)*

Supplies

table salt or sand, black construction paper, wooden toothpicks, small clear glass bottle

Gazillions of Grains

Give each child a piece of black construction paper. Place the paper on a flat surface. Sprinkle salt or sand on each piece.

Ask: What did God promise Abraham and Sarah? *(that their children and grandchildren would be more than the dust of the earth or the stars in the sky)* **How many is that?** *(a lot)* **What did Abraham and Sarah have to do?** *(Be patient and wait for the Lord.)*

Let the children guess the number of salt or sand grains and then spend three minutes counting them. Use a toothpick to separate the grains. Write down whatever total the children give you. Then take all of their grains of salt or sand and fill a small clear glass bottle.

Ask: Do you think Abraham and Sarah are going to have many grandchildren and great-grandchildren and great-great-grandchildren? *(Yes)* **Do think it was hard to wait?** *(yes)* **Did they trust God?** *(yes)*

Supplies

Reproducible 4B, scissors

Surprise! Surprise!

Make enough copies of the animal cards **(Reproducible 4B)** for each child to have an animal card and to create a leader deck (a leader deck is one of each card). Shuffle the cards in the leader deck.

Say: It must have been hard not to know when the promise was going to come true. Imagine how excited they finally were when Sarah discovered she was actually going to have a baby at ninety years of age. Let's play a game where we know and don't know.

Have the children make a circle with their chairs. Select one child to be "IT" and stand in the center of the circle. Remove IT's chair from the circle. Have IT draw a card and hold it up. Then the teacher will draw a second card. The persons holding those cards are to change places. If IT gets one of the seats, then the person without a seat comes to the center and becomes the new IT. If the Surprise card turns up, then everyone must change seats.

Ask: How did it feel to have to wait to see who the second card would be? if you were the first card? if you were IT? if you were part of the rest of the group?

We can be patient and trust in God.

46

Bible Verse Sit-in

Supplies

index cards, felt-tip marker

Write the words *patient*, *wait*, *Lord*, and *act* on index cards, one word per card.

Have the children stand in a circle. Randomly hand out each of the word cards. Have the children recite together the words of today's Bible verse. When you come to a word printed on an index card, the person with the card shouts, "patient!" and then sits down. The next person shouts out "wait" and sits down. Continue until the verse is complete.

Redistribute the cards and repeat one or more times to allow others to participate and to help reinforce the Bible verse.

Say: You had to listen and wait to know when it was your turn to say a word and sit down.

Ask: Can you think of times when you have to wait? (*birthdays, Christmas, for mom or dad to come home from work, summer to come, for special vacations, and so forth*) **Is it easy to wait?** (*no*) **Do you think it was easy for Abraham and Sarah to wait for God to keep the promise?** (*no*) **Do you think they ever wondered if God forgot?** (*maybe*)

Say: But we know that God always keeps promises, no matter how long it takes.

We can be patient and trust in God.

Fruit Basket Prayers

Supplies

Plastic fruit

Have the children stand in a circle. Hold a piece of plastic fruit.

Say: Patience is one of the fruit of the Spirit. Our Bible verse is "Be patient and wait for the LORD to act" (Psalm 37:7, GNT). The Holy Spirit helps us have patience.

Toss the plastic fruit to one of the children in the circle.

Pray: Dear God, we thank you for, (*child's name*). Help (*him or her*) have patience and to trust in you. Amen.

Then have the child toss the plastic fruit to another child. Pray for that child. Continue tossing the fruit around the circle until everyone has had a turn.

God's Promise

Use the star code. Read the Bible verse.

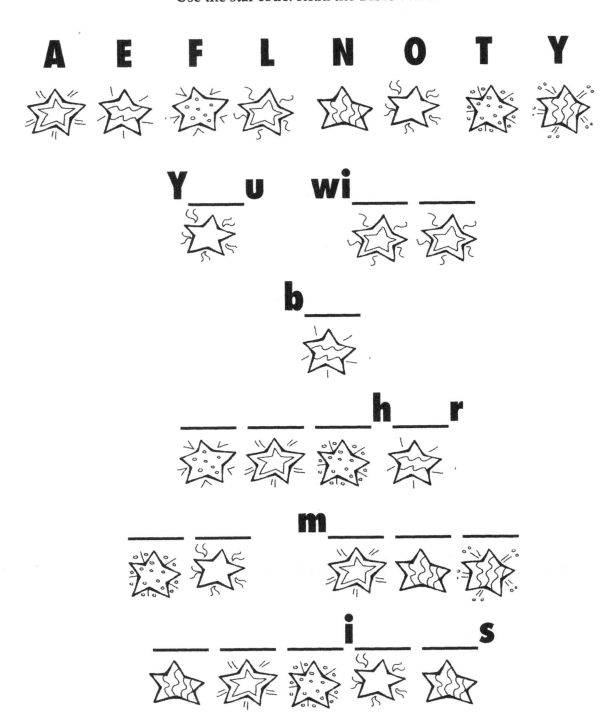

A E F L N O T Y

Y___u wi___ ___

b___

___ ___ ___h ___r

___m___ ___ ___ ___

___ ___ ___i ___ ___s

You can find this promise in Genesis 15:1–6.

ALL-IN-ONE BIBLE FUN

All-in-One
BIBLE ELEMENTARY
FUN

Kindness

Bible Verse

The scripture says, "It is kindness that I want."
Matthew 12:7, GNT

Bible Story

Galatians 5:22–23; Matthew 12:9–14; Mark 3:1–6;
Luke 6:6–11

The story is told in the Gospels of Jesus curing the withered hand of a man on the sabbath. Jesus healed many people during his ministry. His kindness toward all of God's people is shown in the many stories of his love and compassion. However, the healing of the man with the paralyzed hand is an act that angered religious leaders of the day, specifically because Jesus was healing on the sabbath, a day of rest.

Why was this such a problem? Today healing is done routinely every day of the week. Did Jesus merely set aside the laws of the sabbath for more humanitarian purposes?

This story goes straight to the authority of Jesus and his acting in the name of God. Jesus' healing the paralyzed man on the sabbath did not mean that we ignore the laws of God just because this seems to be the right thing to do. Jesus healed the man's withered hand because God has concern and compassion for God's children at all

times. God has shown through Jesus that God's love and compassion for God's children is more important than rituals, even those commanded by God. The old way of doing things was altered to show kindness to one of God's people who greatly needed it. Jesus showed us that God's compassion comes first.

Can we do less as Christians than to follow Jesus' example and show kindness to any of God's people when they need it? Should it matter when they might need our kindness or help? Children naturally reach out to others. Their hearts are easily touched by persons in need. Too often we, as adults, stifle their compassion with our more jaded, pessimistic, and suspicious outlook on society.

Encourage the children to be kind to others. Encourage them to be kind to one another as well. It is more important to be kind than it is to observe all the correct rules of the church.

Be kind to others.

If time is limited, we recommend those activities that are noted in **boldface**. Depending on your time and the number of children, you may be able to include more activities.

ACTIVITY	TIME	SUPPLIES	
Kindness Counts	**5 minutes**	**Reproducible 5A, pencils or crayons**	JOIN THE FUN
Ear-to-Ear Relay	10 minutes	lunch-sized paper bags; crayons, markers, pencils, scissors; paper plate; cookies or crackers; sponges	
May I Come In?	10 minutes	None	BIBLE STORY FUN
Righteous Rules	5 minutes	plastic fruit or other unbreakable item	
Bible Story: What God Requires	**10 minutes**	**None**	
I Can Do That!	10 minutes	Reproducible 5B, masking tape, scissors	
Jump, Turn, Praise!	5 minutes	None	
Vanishing Fruit	5 minutes	index cards, felt-tip marker, tape	LIVE THE FUN
Fruit Basket Prayers	**5 minutes**	**plastic fruit**	

51

Fruit of the Spirit - Elementary

JOIN THE FUN

Supplies

Reproducible 5A, pencils or crayons

Kindness Counts

Make copies of the theme puzzle **(Reproducible 5A)** for today. Place the copies around the room for the children to work on as they arrive.

Welcome the children as they come into the room. Make them each feel a part of the community. Watch for children who need extra kindness today. Encourage members of the group to reach out to them.

Say: Today we are going to talk about kindness, a fruit of the Spirit. Kindness counts. Many children are doing many things in this picture. Find the ones who are not being kind. Ask yourself if you ever do any of those unkind things.

Be kind to others.

Ear-to-Ear Relay

Supplies

lunch-sized paper bags; crayons, markers, pencils, scissors; paper plate; cookies or crackers; sponges

Divide the children into teams of two. Give each team a lunch-sized paper bag and a sponge. Place the objects you will use for the game (pencils, crayons, scissors, markers) around the room in a random fashion.

Say: Since our Bible story today is about being kind and helping, we are going to play a game where each of us has to help our partner. Place the sponge between you, ear-to-ear. Put an arm around either your partner's waist or shoulder. Now, I want you to move about the room collecting one of each of these items: one pencil, one crayon, marker, and one pair of scissors. When the team has one of each of these items, they can trade in the items for two cookies or crackers. Persons who drop the sponge must empty their sacks and start all over again with their partners.

When each child has her or his treat, **ask the children: What did you have to do in order to get the treat for both of you?** (*You had to help each another. One would hold the sack, while the other picked up the item.*)

Be kind to others.

May I Come In?

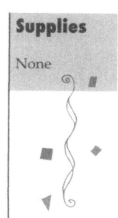
Supplies

None

Say: This morning you have to ask permission before each of you comes to the storytelling area. You must get on your knees, put both hands on top of my hands, and ask, "May I come in?" I will ask, "Then what will you do?" You will tell me some action you will perform. Whisper it in my ear. I will then decide whether or not you can come into the circle.

Place your chair at the entrance to the storytelling area. Have the children one by one come up to the chair, get on their knees, place their hands on top of your hands, and ask, "May I come in?" Respond with, "Then what will you do?" Each child will whisper an action. If it is an act of kindness, allow them to come into the circle. If it is not, send them to the back of the line. Do not give hints as to how those children who are allowed into the circle have gotten there. Give everyone a chance to seek admission.

Ask: What was it that allowed you to come to the circle? (an act of kindness)

> Be kind to others.

Righteous Rules

Supplies

plastic fruit or other un-breakable item

Bring the children together in the storytelling area. Have them sit on the floor. Place a piece of plastic fruit or other unbreakable item from your room (basket, book, box, or other item) on the floor in the center of the circle.

Say: (Call a child by name.) **Bring me the fruit.** (Wait until the child brings the fruit, then have him or her return it to the center of the circle.) (Call a child by name.) **Bring me the fruit but don't touch it with your right hand.** (Wait until the child brings the fruit, then have him or her return it to the center of the circle.) (Call a child by name.) **Bring me the fruit but don't touch it with either hand.** (Continue calling the children and asking them to bring the fruit. Each time make it more restrictive—Don't touch it with your right leg; either leg; don't touch it with any part of your body.)

Ask: As we played the game, what happened? (It got harder and harder until it became impossible to do what was asked.)

Say: Following the rules in today's Bible story became so hard that the rules even kept people from being kind to one another.

What God Requires

by LeeDell Stickler

Say: Today's Bible story tells about a man who for many years had one hand that did not work. This made it very hard for him to work in the fields or care for animals, or even make pottery or leather goods. Jesus took compassion on him and healed him. But the healing meant that Jesus broke one of the laws of the sabbath, according to the Pharisees. They did not see the healing as an act of kindness. Jesus healed the man knowing that he was breaking the rules. He wanted to make a point. It was more important to show kindness to the man than to follow the strict rules which forbid him from working on the sabbath. Being kind is more important to God than all the rituals we can observe.

Divide the children into two groups. One will be the **Pharisees**. *The other group will be the* **Scriptures**. *Let the Pharisees go over their verse until they can say it without looking. When it comes time for their part, let them stand up and shake their fingers at the rest of the class. The Scriptures will speak in a soft whisper. Their response will be a portion of the Bible verse for today.*

Pharisees:
Rules, rules, you gotta keep the rules.
You've got to do exactly what we say.
Rules, rules, you gotta keep the rules.
If you want to celebrate the sabbath day.

Scriptures: But it's kindness that I want.

Don't put your bread in the oven.
Don't bend down to pull out a weed.
Don't go into your wheat field,
And scatter a bag full of seed.
Don't draw from the well any water.
Don't push or pull a wood cart.
Don't move a rock from here to there,
Don't create a great work of art.
Don't swat a fly on the table.
Don't cut a loaf of brown bread.
Don't carry a basket or bundle.
Don't comb the hairs on your head.

Pharisees:
Rules, rules, you gotta keep the rules.
You've got to do exactly what we say.
Rules, rules, you gotta keep the rules.
If you want to celebrate the sabbath day.

Scriptures: But it's kindness that I want.

Don't help a friend who has fallen.
Don't place a cloth on his head.
Don't offer to make him a garment,
Or stitch up a tear with two threads.
Don't kick a ball with your buddies.
Don't drag a stick through the dirt.
Don't tie the strings on your sandals.
Don't try to help one who's hurt.
Don't pluck a grape from a grapevine.
Don't strip any grains from the wheat.
Don't knead, or mix, or stir, or bake
Any food you're planning to eat.

Pharisees:
Rules, rules, you gotta keep the rules.
You've got to do exactly what we say.
Rules, rules, you gotta keep the rules.
If you want to celebrate the sabbath day.

Scriptures: But it's kindness that I want.

If on the sabbath there's someone
Who looks like she needs a good meal.
She'll just have to wait till tomorrow.
That's the rule; that's the way; that's the deal.
If by some chance you are traveling,
There's only so far you may go
If your family wants you to visit,
If they're farther, the answer is "no."
But Jesus knew something was missing.
It was plain as the nose on his face.
People followed the rules without question,
But of something there wasn't a trace.

Pharisees:
Rules, rules, you gotta keep the rules.
You've got to do exactly what we say.
Rules, rules, you gotta keep the rules.
If you want to celebrate the sabbath day.

Scriptures: But it's kindness that I want.

To the synagogue on every sabbath
A man came and sat in the rear.
One of his hands didn't work well
So the crowds, they tried to stay clear.
Jesus wanted to show them
So he called to the man sitting there.
He held out his hand and he beckoned.
"Sir, will you please come up here?"

When the man reached his hand out to Jesus,
His left hand looked just like his right.
He couldn't believe what had happened,
What had happened in plain sight.
Jesus had shown the man kindness,
But the Pharisees threw a big fit.
For Jesus had broken the sabbath
And clearly thought nothing of it.

Pharisees:
Rules, rules, you gotta keep the rules.
You've got to do exactly what we say.
Rules, rules, you gotta keep the rules.
If you want to celebrate the sabbath day.

Scriptures: But it's kindness that I want.

"How much more worth is a person
Than a goat or a cow or a sheep?
It is right to do good on the sabbath.
That's the one rule it's all right to keep."
But the Pharisees muttered and mumbled.
They were angry at what Jesus said.
They whispered together and plotted.
For these men would see Jesus dead.
We know that God's love is for always.
Do good every day of the week.
God wants us live just like Jesus
Showing kindness to all that we meet.
The Scriptures say treat all with kindness.
Don't be afraid to open your heart.
Share all the kindness inside you.
And that's a pretty good start.

Scriptures: But it's kindness that I want.

Supplies

Reproducible 5B, masking tape, scissors

I Can Do That!

Make a copy of the helping tasks (**Reproducible 5B**). There should be one square for each child in the group. Without allowing a child to see what's on the square, use masking tape to attach one to each child's back.

Say: You are wearing a task on your back. It is a task that you can do to help someone else. It is an act of kindness toward someone else. I want you to discover what this task is. You can ask questions about it, but the questions can only be answered with a "yes" or a "no." Does everyone understand? Let's see how many of you can discover your task before I call time.

Give the children ample time to mill around and ask one another enough questions to identify their tasks. When they have discovered what each one's task is, let them move the squares from their backs to their fronts.

Ask: What are some of the tasks that you were wearing on your back? *(cleaning their rooms; walking their dogs; setting the table; vacuuming the carpet; making their beds; fixing their own lunch)* **How many of you do some of these jobs?** *(Invite the children to share.)* **Are there other jobs you do that show kindness to others?**

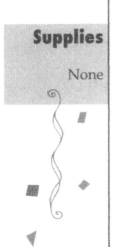

Supplies

None

Jump, Turn, Praise!

Sing the song "Fruit of the Spirit Jump" to the tune of "Pick a Bale of Cotton." Encourage the children to do the motions as they sing together.

Fruit of the Spirit Jump

Gonna jump down, turn around,
(Jump; turn around.)
Show kindness and praise God.
(Put one hand on heart; raise arms.)
Jump down, turn around,
(Jump; turn around.)
Show kindness and praise!
(Put one hand on heart; raise arms.)

Gonna jump down, turn around,
(Jump; turn around.)
Show my peace and praise God.
(Make a peace sign; raise arms.)
Jump down, turn around,
(Jump; turn around.)
Show my peace and praise!
(Make a peace sign; raise arms.)

Gonna jump down, turn around,
(Jump; turn around.)
Show my joy and praise God.
(Pat hands on chest many times; raise arms.)
Jump down, turn around,
(Jump; turn around)
Show my joy and praise!
(Pat hands on chest many times; raise arms.)

Gonna jump down, turn around,
(Jump; turn around.)
Show my love and praise God.
(Cross arms over chest; raise arms.)
Jump down, turn around,
(Jump; turn around.)
Show my love and praise!
(Cross arms over chest; raise arms.)

© 2001 Abingdon Press

56

Vanishing Fruit

Supplies

index cards, felt-tip marker, tape

Write the word "kindness" on index cards, one letter per card.

Tape the index cards on a wall or set them on a table in order of the word.

Say: Kindness is a fruit of the Spirit. We learn through the Bible that Jesus wants us to be kind to others. I want you to see if you can come up with one act of kindness that begins with each letter of this fruit of the Spirit. I will give you the letter. Let's see if we can make the word disappear and come up with some ways that we can show kindness to others.

As each child comes up with an act of kindness that begins with one of the letters of the word "kindness," remove that letter from the wall or table. When every letter is removed, encourage the children to cheer.

Be kind to others.

Fruit Basket Prayers

Supplies

plastic fruit

Have the children stand in a circle. Hold a piece of plastic fruit.

Say: Kindness is one of the fruit of the Spirit. Jesus taught the people that acting religious and following all the rules doesn't count if they weren't kind to one another.

Toss the plastic fruit to one of the children in the circle.

Pray: Dear God, we thank you for (child's name). Help (him or her) show kindness to others. Amen.

Then have the child toss the plastic fruit to another child. Pray for that child. Continue tossing the fruit around the circle until everyone has had a turn.

Be Kind!

God wants us to be kind.
Put an "X" on all of those who are not being kind.

The scripture says, "It is kindness that I want." (Matthew 12:7, GNT)

Set the table.

Clean my room.

Vacuum the carpet.

Fix my lunch.

Make my bed.

Walk the dog.

Generosity

Bible Verse

For God loves a cheerful giver.

2 Corinthians 9:7

Bible Story

Galatians 5:22–23; Mark 12:41–44; Luke 21:1–4

What makes a person generous? What is the true measure of a gift? These are questions that can be addressed by looking at the story of the widow's coins.

Outside of the Temple were thirteen receptacles to receive the gifts of the worshippers. There would be a loud clanging noise when the coins dropped. One day, Jesus had been sitting watching people drop coins into these receptacles. He would have had to hear all the noise these contributions made. When the poor widow arrived and put her two copper coins into one of the receptacles, it would have been easy to "hear" that her contribution was very small.

The two copper coins were the smallest of the denominations of coins. They had very little value. And yet the widow gave with her heart all that she had. These coins probably represented her next meal. The rich who had been dropping large quantities of coins into the receptacles were giving out of their abundance. They could still afford large meals, lavish homes, and richly designed clothing. The widow would have none of these things, even if she kept her money. But the widow gave to God even that which she needed, while the rich gave of their extra.

Jesus did not condemn the gift of the wealthy, of the extra. What Jesus did was to commend the extreme generosity of heart that caused the widow to give all she had to God. This generosity demonstrates a truly selfless way of living for us.

No gift of love is too small to count, and sharing what we have and who we are with complete unselfishness does not go unnoticed by God. Even the smallest gift can be the most generous gift. It depends upon the heart.

Be a generous and cheerful giver.

If time is limited, we recommend those activities that are noted in **boldface**. Depending on your time and the number of children, you may be able to include more activities.

ACTIVITY	TIME	SUPPLIES	
Treasury Search	**5 minutes**	**Reproducible 6A, pencils or crayons**	JOIN THE FUN
Just for Grins	10 minutes	drawing paper, crayons or felt-tip markers, scissors, masking tape	
Put on a Happy Face	10 minutes	Reproducible 6B, large brown paper grocery bags, masking tape, blindfolds, individual grins (from "Just for Grins")	BIBLE STORY FUN
Bible Story: The More Generous Gift	**10 minutes**	**different colored highlighters, courtroom setup, gavel, judge's robe**	
Clink! Clank! Clunk!	10 minutes	metal baking pan, coins or metal washers, basket or bowl	
Cheerful Signs	5 minutes	coins or metal washers, metal pan	LIVE THE FUN
Fruit Basket Prayer	**5 minutes**	**plastic fruit**	

JOIN THE FUN

Treasury Search

Make a copy of the hidden coin puzzle **(Reproducible 6A)** for each child.

Welcome the children as they arrive. Give each child a copy of the hidden coin puzzle.

Say: In Bible times the people came into the Temple treasury to give their offerings of money. There in front of them were thirteen boxes where they could place their coins. One by one they would put the coins in the box. This represented their offering to God. Now, however, someone has lost all the coins from the boxes. See how many coins you can find. *(There are ten coins.)*

Be a generous and cheerful giver.

Just for Grins

Give each child a piece of drawing paper and crayons or markers to complete the assignment.

Say: Today's Bible verse is "God loves a cheerful giver." Say it with me. *(Have the children repeat the Bible verse.)* **This means that God wants each of us to be: not a grouchy giver, not a sleepy giver, not a silly giver, but a cheerful giver.**

Ask: What does your mouth look like when you are cheerful? Can you show me now? *(Wait until all the children are making cheerful smiles.)*

Say: We are going to play a game, but what we need first are cheerful grins. On your drawing paper, I want each of you to create a cheerful grin. Cut it out and put your name on the back.

When everyone has finished making their grins, have the children come together in the storytelling area. Put a loop of masking tape on the back of each grin.

Put on a Happy Face

Supplies

Reproducible 6B, large brown paper grocery bags, masking tape, blindfolds, individual grins (from "Just for Grins" activity)

Divide the children into teams of three members. Make a copy of the Happy Face **(Reproducible 6B)**. Tape one face to the front of a large brown paper grocery bag, one for each team.

Let each member of the team decide whether he or she will be "A," "B," or "C."

"A" will be the placer whose job it is to put the grin on the face.
"B" will be the guide whose job it is to tell the placer where to put the grin on the face.
"C" will be the face. The person who is playing the face will be wearing the grocery sack over his or her head. (Caution: Be sensitive to children who may be claustrophobic and unable to wear the grocery bag. Allow these children to be either guides or placers.)

Say: Your job is to "put on a happy face" because God loves a (pause and let the children fill in the words) **"cheerful giver." When I say "Go!" each team will have one chance to place their grins on their happy faces. The locations on the face that a child touches are where the grins will be stuck. The only catch is that "A" will be blindfolded. "B" will give "A" directions on how far to walk and in which direction to walk. "C" will wait to be happy.**

Bring all the team members who are playing "As" to a starting point about ten feet away from their other team members. Blindfold the "As." "Bs" will stand behind "As" and give verbal directions, but will not touch "As" in any way. "Cs" will stand across the room, hands down at their sides.

Make sure the area is clear of any obstructions the children might trip over or run into.

When each of the teams has placed its grin, let the children share their Happy Faces. If you have time, let the children rotate. "As" will become the guides, "Bs" the faces, and "Cs" the placers.

Be a generous and cheerful giver.

The More Generous Gift

by LeeDell Stickler

Make a copy of the script for each of the characters. Highlight each part with a different-colored marker. Create a courtroom in the class: a judge's bench, witness chair, two podiums, and the audience. Invite children who are confident readers to read the parts or invite youth from another age level to be the characters. Give them the scripts in advance. You will need these characters: Court Clerk, Judge Wright, Rich Man, Jesus, Disciple, Citizen, Widow.

Say: Welcome to Court. Today we will hear the case of the rich man versus Jesus. Listen carefully and at the end cast your vote: Was the rich man's gift a more generous gift? or was the widow's contribution greater?

Court Clerk: Court is now in session. The honorable Judge I. M. Wright is presiding. *(Judge comes in and takes her or his seat.)*

Judge Wright: *(bangs gavel)* Will the two complainants please step forward? *(Jesus and the Rich Man stand behind their podiums.)*

Judge Wright: And just why are we in the courtroom today?

Rich Man: I'm tired of being the bad guy. It just isn't fair. I want it stopped. *(Pounds fist on the podium.)*

Judge Wright: Jesus, would you like to answer that?

Jesus: I didn't say he was a bad guy. I was just pointing out to my disciples that the widow had given a greater gift than he did.

Rich Man: I object, your honor. That isn't a true statement.

Judge Wright: Call your witness.

Rich Man: I call Citizen to the stand.

(Citizen comes forward. The Clerk meets her or him and swears the person in.)

Clerk: Do you promise to tell the truth, the whole truth, and nothing but the truth? *(Citizen says "I do.")* Please be seated.

Rich Man: Please tell us what happened that day.

Citizen: I came to the Temple to offer prayers. As I passed by the

ALL-IN-ONE BIBLE FUN

treasury, I saw you standing at one of the offering boxes. You had a pouch full of gold coins. One at a time you placed them in the box.

Rich Man: You see, a pouch full of gold, I repeat *gold*, coins.

Judge Wright: Jesus, do you have any questions for the witness?

Jesus: No questions, your honor. I agree that Rich Man put in many gold coins. I never questioned that.

Judge Wright: Then what is your point, Rich Man?

Rich Man: I can make my point if you let me call one more witness. I call one of Jesus' disciples.

(Disciple comes to the front. He is sworn in by the Court Clerk and sits.)

Rich Man: Now, I want you to tell us what your teacher said that day.

Disciple: Jesus said that the widow's gift was much greater than yours because she gave all she had.

Rich Man: There we have it! Her tiny gift was greater than mine!

Jesus: I can clear this up with my next witness. I call the widow.

(The widow comes to the front and is sworn in by the Clerk.)

Jesus: Please tell us what happened on that day in the Temple.

Widow: I came to the Temple to say prayers and give my offering.

Jesus: How much did you put in the box?

Widow: I put in two copper coins.

Rich Man: *(Jumps up.)* See? What did I tell you? That's hardly worth a single penny!

Judge Wright: Sit down, sir.

Jesus: And how much do you have at home to buy food?

Widow: I have nothing left, sir.

Jesus: And Rich Man, how much do you have at home to buy food?

Rich Man: All I need and more.

Jesus: And that is why her gift is a more generous gift. She gave all she had. You gave only what you could spare.

Invite the children to vote either for the rich man or for Jesus. Ask the children to give reasons for their decisions.

BIBLE STORY FUN

Supplies

metal baking pan, coins or metal washers, basket or bowl

Clink! Clank! Clunk!

Have the children move their chairs into a semicircle facing a table or an empty chair.

Provide coins or metal washers to equal the number of children in your group. Place half of the coins on the table or in the seat of the chair. Put the other half of the coins in a bowl or basket placed near the metal baking pan.

Split the class into two groups. Let each group number off. If there is an uneven number of children let the additional person have one of the numbers from earlier in the line.

Say: Outside the Jewish Temple in Bible times were thirteen boxes to receive the gifts of the worshippers. There would be loud clanging noises when the coins dropped into the boxes. One day, Jesus had been sitting and watching people drop coins into these boxes. He would have had to hear all the noise these contributions made. Surely the rich people were aware of the noise their contributions made and probably made the most of this to enhance their own importance. When the poor widow arrived and put her two copper coins in one of the boxes, it would have been easy to "hear" that her contribution was very small. She was probably embarrassed that she had so little to give.

Continue: Let's play a game. I am going to drop coins into this metal pan. Count the number of coins I drop. If the number of coins is the same as your number, you will rush to the front and grab a coin from the chair or table and come back to your seat. However, there are two (and maybe three) people who have that number. The first person who gets the coin gets to return to her or his seat. The person who is last gets to be the coin dropper on the next round.

If you have children who have physical disabilities, this game would not be appropriate. If you have children who are hard of hearing, adapt the game so that the numbers are held up rather than forcing the children to have to strain to catch the noises.

Say: Jesus didn't say the gifts of the rich were not good gifts; he only said the widow's gift was the more generous gift because she gave all she had.

Be a generous and cheerful giver.

Cheerful Signs

Have the children sit down in your worship area. Teach the children the Bible verse using signs from American Sign Language.

God loves a cheerful giver.

Say: Today's fruit of the Spirit word is generosity.

Ask: There were two people in today's Bible story who gave an offering. Who was the more generous? *(the widow)* Why? *(She gave all that she had.)*

Say: Being generous doesn't always mean giving money. Sometimes it means giving time and services to others. You might take time to help at home when you'd rather be outside playing *(toss a coin or metal washer to one of the children and have him or her put the coin or washer in his or her lap and then sign the Bible verse)*, or explain how to do a math problem to someone else instead of doing your own homework *(toss a coin to another child and have her or him sign the Bible verse.)*

Continue with examples until each of the children has a coin. Then pass around the metal pan and let the children drop their coins inside.

Fruit Basket Prayers

Have the children stand in a circle. Hold a piece of plastic fruit.

Say: Generosity is one of the fruit of the Spirit. When the Holy Spirit lives in you, you are generous to others.

Toss the plastic fruit to one of the children in the circle.

Pray: Dear God, we thank you for *(child's name)*. Help *(her or him)* to be generous with time and with money. Amen.

Then have the child toss the plastic fruit to another child. Pray for that child. Continue tossing the fruit around the circle until everyone has had a turn.

Treasury Search

  For God loves a cheerful giver. (2 Corinthians 9:7)

ALL-IN-ONE BIBLE FUN

Fruit of the Spirit - Elementary

All-in-One BIBLE FUN ELEMENTARY

Faithfulness

Bible Verse

Do everything God commands, and be faithful to God.

Deuteronomy 11:22, GNT

Bible Story

Galatians 5:22–23; 2 Kings 22:1–24:5

The Southern Kingdom of Judah was ruled by the house of David until Judah fell to the Babylonians sometime around 587 B.C. Josiah, who reigned from about 640 to 609 B.C., became king when he was eight years old. Some time in his twenties, Josiah began to make his own decisions. Josiah looked around and saw that the worship practices of Assyria had, over time, influenced the worship practices of his people. These worship practices did not reflect what God intended worship to be.

Now, Josiah, unlike most of Judah's kings, was faithful to God. Josiah ordered that the Temple at Jerusalem be repaired. During the restoration of the Temple, some form of the Book of Deuteronomy was discovered (probably chapters 12–26 of our present book of Deuteronomy). Deuteronomy was the Book of Jewish Law.

Huldah the prophetess verified the authenticity of the scrolls and Josiah called the people together to hear the words of the Law and for them to renew their covenant with God. The discovery of this Book of Law helped Josiah to reform the practices of the Hebrew people. Josiah established the Temple in Jerusalem as the central place of worship and reinstated the celebration of Passover.

Faithfulness to God set Josiah apart from the other kings of Judah and even from his own people. Josiah attempted to bring his people back to faithfulness to the God of the covenant, not to following the general fads of the culture around them.

What does it mean to be faithful to God today? Does it mean going to church? praying and reading the Bible? performing acts of service? witnessing to others about Jesus? The answer to each of these questions is "Yes!"—that and so much more. Being faithful to God and standing against pressure to conform to the fads of the day isn't easy; it never was.

Be faithful to God and obey God's commandments.

If time is limited, we recommend those activities that are noted in **boldface**. Depending on your time and the number of children, you may be able to include more activities.

ACTIVITY	TIME	SUPPLIES
Excavation Adventure	**5 minutes**	**Reproducible 7A, crayons or pencils**
In Like Me	10 minutes	None
Can You Dig It?	10 minutes	Reproducible 7B, tape, newspaper, basket or bag
Bible Story: Josiah and the Hidden Scrolls	**10 minutes**	**brown paper, felt-tip pen, yarn**
Pictured Parchments	10 minutes	brown wrapping paper, scissors, Bible, yarn, permanent felt-tip markers or crayons, plastic dishpan partially filled with water, iron, newspaper, large piece of paper, examples of illuminated manuscripts
Fractured Scriptures	10 minutes	index cards, felt-tip marker, envelopes, scissors
Fruit Basket Prayers	**10 minutes**	**plastic fruit**

JOIN THE FUN

BIBLE STORY FUN

LIVE THE FUN

71

JOIN THE FUN

Supplies

Reproducible 7A, crayons or pencils

Excavation Adventure

Make a copy of the maze puzzle **(Reproducible 7A)** for each child.

Say: In today's Bible story we will make an exciting discovery. Some workers come across a secret hiding place while excavating the ruins of the Hebrew Temple in Jerusalem. The workers find a clay jar in this hiding place. The workers find some scrolls that had been hidden away for many, many years inside the clay jar. These scrolls have a message for the people who read them. These scrolls tell the people what they have to do in order to be faithful to God. See if you can discover which worker found the scrolls. *(Worker C)*

> **Be faithful to God and obey God's commandments.**

Supplies

None

In Like Me

Bring the children together in an open area of the room. Make sure there is plenty of space for movement.

Say: Every year there are new fads. We have to think like "this." We have to wear "that." We have to listen to "this." We have to say "that" in order to be cool. Every generation does the same thing. Let's play a game to see just how silly we can be in order to be "IN."

Teach the children this simple poem:
> **Lend an ear! Look and see!**
> **This is what it takes to be IN like me.**

Start with the child on your right. That child will say the poem and then decide on an action, such as: "Walk like a duck;" "Talk with a squeaky voice;" "Waggle your head back and forth;" "Shake a leg;" and so forth. Then everyone in the group has to copy that action. The second person in line does the same thing, but adds another action. Now the whole class is doing two actions in order to be IN. Continue around the circle until everyone has had a chance to suggest an action.

Ask: Have you ever wondered who decides what is IN and what is not? Who decides what clothes are cool and which ones are not? *(Invite the children to discuss this.)*

Can You Dig It?

Supplies

Reproducible 7B, tape, newspaper, basket or bag

Prior to class, copy the discovered objects page **(Reproducible 7B)**. Cut each apart, roll it into a small scroll, and tape. Make several copies of the discovered objects page if you have a large class. Place the scrolls in a basket or bag until time for this activity.

Have the children arrange their chairs in a circle. Give the children stacks of newspaper and let them crumple newspaper into balls. Throw the newspaper balls into the center of the circle. Keep crumpling balls until the center is filled. When the center is filled so that no floor is showing, sprinkle the small scrolls over the surface and walk through it to mix it up.

Say: We are going on a archaeological dig. King Josiah in today's Bible story sent workmen to restore the Temple, which was run down from neglect. It was in need of repair. As the workers dug through the rubble they found something important. Somewhere in all of this rubble are small scrolls. Whenever you find a small scroll, you'll hold it up and shout: "I found something!" Say it just as though you were one of those scientists who dig through old ruins. Everyone must then freeze where they are and ask: "What did you find?" The person who found the scroll will unroll it and share what she or he found. If a person finds a family of bats, a nest of rats, some broken clay lamps, a spider web, some old gold coins, a few pottery shards, a pile of animal bones, or a nest of snakes, everyone will say "Awww." Then they will return to looking. Place the discovered item in the basket or bag.

Continue: The fun comes, however, when someone finds the clay jars with the scrolls inside. Everyone will jump up and run back to the circle when the finder reads what is in the little scroll; they will try not to be the last person to get a seat. The last person who gets to his or her chair must sing a song that the group chooses.

Remind the children that the scrolls the workmen found contained a special book of the Bible called Deuteronomy. This book contained many of the laws that God gave the people, laws that the people had forgotten.

> ### Be faithful to God and obey God's commandments.

Have the children work together after the game to pick up all the newspaper balls to recycle.

Josiah and the Hidden Scrolls

by LeeDell Stickler

Make seventeen brown paper scrolls. Write one of the rules from the Book of Deuteronomy on each scroll. Tie each scroll with yarn and placed these under each chair in the story-telling center. If you usually have more than seventeen children, reference Deuteronomy and choose additional commands.

1. You shall have no other gods before me.
2. Do not make and bow down to idols.
3. Do not use God's name in a bad way.
4. Set aside the seventh day of the week for rest and dedicate it to God.
5. Respect your father and mother.
6. Do not commit murder.
7. Be faithful to your husband or wife.
8. Do not steal.
9. Do not tell lies against your neighbor.
10. Do not want what others have.
11. Love the Lord your God with all your heart and soul and might.
12. Give a part of what you grow or earn to God.
13. Every seventh year you shall forgive the debts of those who owe you.
14. Keep the Passover at its appointed time.
15. Celebrate the Festival of Weeks and make an offering of what you've earned.
16. Keep the Festival of Booths for 7 days.
17. All the males shall come to the Temple three times a year to show loyalty to God.

Say: Today our Bible story is about a boy who became king when he was only eight years old. His name was Josiah and he wanted to be the very best king he could be. During his reign something was discovered that changed the people of his king-dom. I will point to you at a certain place in the story. Reach under your chair and remove the scroll that is there. Read it to the group, or ask me to help you read it.

Josiah was eight years old when he became the king of Judah. Even though he was young, Josiah was faithful to God. As Josiah grew, he listened and learned. One of the things he learned was that the people had begun to follow ways that were not faithful to God.

"How can they know what God requires if they have no place to worship God?" thought Josiah. So Josiah decided to repair the Temple of Jerusalem. He put men to work clearing out the rubble that had filled the Temple.

One day Josiah sent his secretary Shapan (SHAY fuhn) to the Temple to pay the workers. No sooner had he arrived than Hilkiah (hil KI uh) the priest came running out to him.

ALL-IN-ONE BIBLE FUN

"Look what some workers have found!" Hilkiah held out a large scroll. "This appears to be a book of law. Take this to the king and let him decide what to do." Hilkiah handed the scroll to Shapan.

Shapan hurried back to the palace and presented the scroll to the king. "See, King Josiah. It is the lost Book of Law! Some workmen have uncovered in the Temple."

King Josiah carefully unrolled the scroll and began to read. *(Point to one child.)* As he read he became quite troubled. *(Point to another child.)* His brow crinkled. *(Point to another child.)* His beard twitched. *(Point to another child.)* His eyes blinked. *(Point to another child.)* And he scratched his chin. *(Point to another child.)*

"My people have not seen this scroll for many years. Some of the rules that are written here have never been heard before. My people are being unfaithful to God and they don't even know it! But before we make this known to the people, we must make sure this is real."

So Hilkiah and Shapan took the scroll to Huldah (HUHL duh), who was a prophetess. She would know if these words were real.

Huldah carefully unrolled the scroll and began to read. *(Point to another child.)* As she read, she became quite troubled. *(Point to another child.)* Her brow crinkled. *(Point to another child.)* Her eyes blinked. *(Point to another child.)* Her nose twitched. *(Point to another child.)* She scratched her chin. *(Point to another child.)*

"Oh, yes," Huldah said. "These are the words of God. This is the lost book of the Law of Moses. Truly the people have not been living by these laws. But God will give them another chance because King Josiah is sorry and is willing to change. But from now on the people will have to do what these words say."

So Josiah called all the people together. He began to read the words of the long lost law. The people listened carefully. *(Point to another child.)* They became quite troubled. *(Point to another child.)* Their brows crinkled. *(Point to another child.)* Their ears twitched. *(Point to another child.)* Their eyes blinked. *(Point to another child.)* And they scratched their heads. *(Point to another child.)* But they all agreed that they needed to live in a different way. So all the people joined in the promise. They would be faithful to God. They would live by God's commands.

Pictured Parchments

Supplies

brown wrap-
ping paper,
scissors, Bible,
yarn, perma-
nent felt-tip
markers or
crayons, plas-
tic dishpan
partially filled
with water,
iron,
newspaper,
large piece of
paper, exam-
ples of illumi-
nated
manuscripts

Cut brown wrapping paper into pieces about twenty-two inches wide by twelve inches high. Place a plastic dishpan partially filled with water on a table covered with newspaper. Set up an ironing board and iron away from foot traffic areas. Use this with adult supervision only.

Say: **The scrolls that the workmen found were parts of the Book of Deuteronomy, the fifth book of the Bible.**

Show the children where Deuteronomy can be found in the Bible.

Say: **This book of the Bible contains laws that tell people what God requires of them in order that they be the people of God. When the people discovered these laws they wanted to obey them. They wanted to be God's people. Today we read the Bible to discover what God wants us to do. Even before there were printing presses, people copied the books of the Bible so that others could read them. Every generation wants the next generation to know what it takes to be faithful to God.**

Show examples of illuminated manuscripts from medieval times. (Libraries are good sources for these. You can also find pages of illuminated manuscripts on the Internet.) Set out the manuscripts where the children can look at them. Point out that the people who made these illustrations wanted readers to know how special and important she or he thought these words were.

Ask: **What are some things the Bible tells us that we can do to be faithful to God?**

Write the children's suggestions on a large sheet of paper. Do not make an exhaustive list, but write enough that the children will have several ways to choose from in which they can be faithful.

Say: **Today we are going to make illuminated scrolls to take home to remind us what we can do to be faithful to God. Choose one or more of the suggestions from our list and write it on the scroll. Then illustrate the manuscript just as the scribes and monks did so long ago.**

Have the children do the writing and illustrating with permanent felt-tip markers or with crayons. Then crumple the scroll into a ball, and dip it in water. Squeeze the excess water out and open the scroll carefully. Then place the opened scroll between two sheets of newspaper. Iron until dry. Roll into a scroll. Tie with yarn.

Say: **The words of the Bible help us to know how to be faithful to God.**

Fractured Scriptures

Supplies

index cards, felt-tip marker, envelopes, scissors

Write the complete Bible verse, "Do everything God commands, and be faithful to God" (Deuteronomy 11:22, GNT) on several index cards. Cut the words apart or in different combinations. Put each combination in an envelope.

Divide the children into teams of two or three members. Give each team an envelope with the fractured scriptures. See which teams can get their scriptures finished. To keep this from becoming a contest, tell children the game won't be over until everyone has finished. Let teams that have finished help those who are still working.

Fruit Basket Prayers

Supplies

plastic fruit

Have the children stand in a circle. Hold a piece of plastic fruit.

Ask: Who wants to guess what the fruit of the Spirit word is for today? *(Invite the children to guess. Accept "faithful" or "faithfulness.")*

> Be faithful to God and obey God's commandments.

Say: Name something someone might do to show that he or she is faithful to God. If everyone agrees that the action is faithful, everyone will say the Bible verse together: "Do everything God commands, and be faithful to God" (Deuteronomy 11:22, GNT). If everyone thinks the action is not faithful, stay silent.

Be ready to name several activities yourself. For example cheating on a test *(stay silent)*; **helping a friend with homework** *(Bible verse)*; **going to Sunday school** *(Bible verse)*; **forgetting to say your prayers** *(stay silent)*).

Toss the plastic fruit to one of the children in the circle.

Pray: Dear God, we thank you for *(child's name)*. **Help** *(him or her)* **be faithful to you and obey your commandments. Amen.**

Then have the child toss the plastic fruit to another child. Pray for that child. Continue tossing the fruit around the circle until everyone has had a turn.

Which worker found the hidden scrolls?

REPRODUCIBLE 7A

ALL-IN-ONE BIBLE FUN

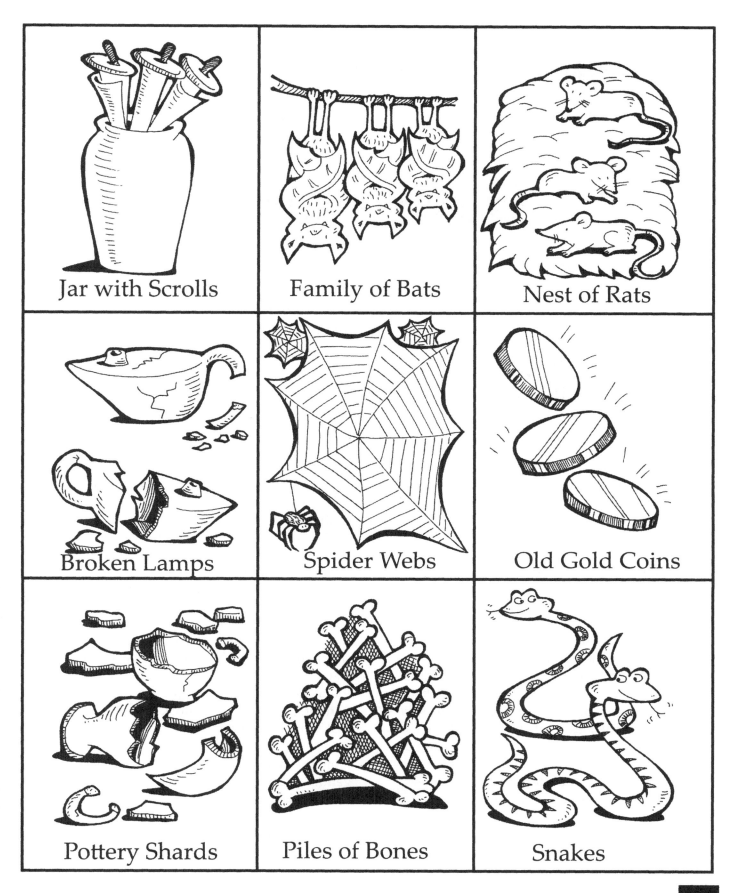

Jar with Scrolls

Family of Bats

Nest of Rats

Broken Lamps

Spider Webs

Old Gold Coins

Pottery Shards

Piles of Bones

Snakes

Gentleness

Bible Verse

Let your gentleness be known to everyone.

Philippians 4:5

Bible Story

Galatians 5:22–23; Psalm 23

Who would question that the Twenty-third Psalm is the most-often-quoted Old Testament Scripture passage? This psalm provides quiet assurance during times of crisis and chaos. Its words soothe the soul and remind us we belong to God.

In this psalm we see God as the caring shepherd who is responsible for caring for the defenseless. Sheep, naturally stupid and willful animals, need great care. They are easily led astray. They eat things that are not good for them. They are virtually defenseless against predatory animals. A shepherd's care gives sheep a much better chance of survival. We recognize ourselves in these verses. God attempts to keep God's people on the straight path, chastising us when we do not do what is good for ourselves; and protecting us from those things that we do to each other.

The images in Psalm 23 show how God demonstrates a gentle, caring, nurturing relationship with God's people. God makes us "lie down in green pastures." (We need rest; God gives us the Sabbath.) God leads us in "right paths." (We are such willful sheep that God reaches out to us constantly so that we do not become lost to God.) And God walks with us "through the darkest valley" (God is with us even in the bad times.) If we allow God to treat us gently, then God will care for all our needs.

When we treat others lovingly and gently we are treating them just as the great shepherd in Psalm 23 treats the sheep, and just as God treats us. The best way for us to thank God for God's care and gentleness is to treat the rest of God's flock (people) with that same gentleness.

How do we instill in the children a sense of gentleness? We begin early and show them that displays of physical strength are not necessary to achieve the important goals of life. Jesus was a gentle man, but he was never a wimp. It takes a strong person to have a gentle demeanor.

We can treat others with gentleness.

If time is limited, we recommend those activities that are noted in **boldface**. Depending on your time and the number of children, you may be able to include more activities.

ACTIVITY	TIME	SUPPLIES	
A Gentle Touch	**5 minutes**	**Reproducible 8A, crayons or felt-tip markers**	JOIN THE FUN
On the Right Path	10 minutes	masking tape, blindfolds for half the class, small pad of sticky notes	
Wonderful Words	10 minutes	index cards, felt-tip markers (red, blue, green, purple), construction paper (red, blue, green, purple), bag or basket	BIBLE STORY FUN
Bible Story: Gentle Shepherd	**10 minutes**	**white paper plates, black construction paper, stapler and staples, wooden pole, scissors**	
To the Rescue!	10 minutes	Reproducible 8B, scissors, crayons or felt-tip markers, pennies or metal washers, tray or cardboard, stapler and staples, scraps of paper, plastic drinking straws, masking tape	
No Wimps Allowed!	5 minutes	paper birds from "To the Rescue!" activity (Reproducible 8B)	LIVE THE FUN
Fruit Basket Prayers	**10 minutes**	**plastic fruit**	

81

A Gentle Touch

Supplies

Reproducible 8A, crayons or felt-tip markers

Make a copy of the gentle picture puzzle **(Reproducible 8A)** for each child. Greet the children in a warm fashion. Model a gentle demeanor for the children to follow.

Have the children find the different items pictured in the puzzle. Then let the children color the picture.

Ask: What kinds of things do you think of when you hear the word *gentle*? (*Let the children name some things.*)

Say: Today's fruit of the Spirit is gentleness. We don't often think about being gentle as being part of what the Holy Spirit brings into our lives.

We can treat others with gentleness.

On the Right Path

Supplies

masking tape, blindfolds for half the class, small pad of sticky notes

Use masking tape to mark a trail around the center of the room. Make sure the trail is no wider than two feet. Provide turns in the trail that will require careful negotiation.

Select one of the children to be the marshal. If this creates an uneven number of children, let two children be marshals and station them on opposite sides of the game field. Divide the remaining children into teams of two. Give each team a blindfold. Have the team members decide who is going to be the Trailwalker and who is going to be the Guide.

Say: Today we will participate in a kind of Trust Walk. Instead of one person leading the other through the course, one person is going to guide the other person—not with words, but with a gentle touch on either the person's right or left shoulder. This will direct the Trailwalker in the appropriate direction. A touch on the right shoulder means turn to the right. A touch on the left shoulder means turn to the left. A touch in the center of the back means to go straight ahead. The marshal will say, "You're out!" if anyone steps outside the trail, and that team will then be handed a ticket (*small sticky note*)**. Let's try to walk down the path without collecting any tickets. The team with the fewest wins.**

When the first player has made it down the right path, then have the children switch places.

Wonderful Words

Supplies

index cards, felt-tip markers (red, blue, green, purple), construction paper (red, blue, green, purple), bag or basket

Bring the children together in the storytelling area. Set out these colors of felt-tip markers for each child or pair of children: red, blue, green, and purple. Give each child four blank index cards.

Place squares of colored construction paper (blue, green, red, purple) in four different areas of the room. Tape the paper to the floor so that it will not move if stepped on. Make sure there is plenty of space around the paper square where children may stand.

Say: Even though words are only squiggly marks written on paper or sounds that come from our lips, words can be very powerful. Words can make us happy. Words can make us sad. Words can hurt our feelings. Words can make us angry. Words can make us feel safe and welcome.

We are going to make a collection of words. I want each of you to write a word that makes you feel happy. Use a purple marker to write it on one of the cards. (*Give the children time to write their words. Don't worry about spelling.*) **With the blue marker write a word that makes you feel sad.** (*Give the children time to write their words.*) **Write a word with the red marker that makes you feel angry.** (*Give the children time to write their words.*) **Write a word with the green marker that makes you feel calm.** (*Give the children time to write their words.*)

Collect all the index cards and put them in a bag or basket.

Say: I am going to draw out one of the words and read it. If you think this word is an angry word, go stand beside the red square. If you think this word is a happy word, go stand beside the purple square. If you think the word is a sad word, go stand beside the blue square. If you think the word is a calm word, go stand beside the green square.

Draw the index cards from the bag or basket, one at a time. Let the children vote. Do not be surprised if some of the children assign other meanings to the words than those given by the original writer. Invite the children to explain their feelings about some of the words.

 We can treat others with gentleness.

Gentle Shepherd

by LeeDell Stickler

Cut slits from the edges of two white paper plates, to the center points. Overlap slightly so the plates become wide cones. Cut two ears from black construction paper and staple to the paper plates. These are the sheep hats. Select one or two children to be the sheep. Place the sheep hats on each child's head. Choose one person to be the shepherd. Give that child a wooden pole. Stand the shepherd near the sheep. Another child can be the lion. Have that child hide behind chairs, waiting for sheep.

Say: Today's Bible story is known as the Twenty-third Psalm. Some people call it the Shepherd's psalm. It's also called a psalm of David. The psalm talks about a shepherd and his sheep. Here we have a shepherd *(put hand on the head of child selected to be the shepherd)*, **and some sheep** *(pat the sheep's heads and encourage them to say "baa.")*

Continue: The Bible-times shepherd was a very responsible person. *(Walk over to the shepherd. Have him or her stand up very straight.)* **The shepherd had to be very strong.** *(Have the child make muscle arms)*, **and very brave** *(have child look fierce)*. **Sheep, on the other hand, were not very smart. They depended upon shepherds to take care of them. They followed this shepherd wherever she or he went.** *(Have the shepherd walk and the sheep follow.)* **Sometimes the sheep would try to wander away.** *(Have sheep wander away.)* **But the shepherd would always bring them back. Sometimes the sheep would get stuck in rocks or their wool would be caught in thorn bushes.** *(Have the sheep pretend to get stuck.)* **But the shepherd rescued them.** *(Have the shepherd rescue the sheep.)*

Continue: Sometimes a lion or a bear or a wolf would try to have lamb chops for dinner. *(Have the lion attack the sheep.)* **But the shepherd would use his staff or a sling to protect them.** *(Have the shepherd get between the sheep and the lion. Have the lion run away.)* **Sheep were also very stubborn animals. A shepherd might lead them to water, but if it were rushing by too fast, the sheep would not drink.** *(Have the shepherd lead the sleep to a pool of water and have the sheep turn their noses up.)* **So the shepherd would have to dip his bucket into the stream, dig a trough, and give the sheep water.**

Say: Our Bible lesson compares the shepherd to God and the sheep to us. Just as the shepherd takes good care of the sheep, God also takes good care of us. I will read a line or two of the psalm. Then I will add sentences that should help us to understand what the psalm means to us today. When I say those parts, I will hold up my hand and you will repeat it after me, just as I say it.

The LORD is my shepherd, I shall not want.
God gives me good food to eat:
    cereal and juice;
    peanut butter and jelly;
    pizza and ice cream and spinach.
God gives me a place to live.
God gives me friends and family.
God gives me clothes to wear.

He makes me lie down in green pastures; he leads me beside still waters;
God watches over me
    when I get up;
    when I'm at school;
    when I play with my friends;
    when I am doing my homework;
    when I go to sleep at night.

he restores my soul.
God knows my feelings
    when I'm angry;
    when I'm sad;
    when I'm out of sorts;
And I don't feel so lonely.

He leads me in right paths for his name's sake.
God is like a teacher who helps me
    do what's right;
    be kind to others;
    remember to say "please" and
        "thank you";
    share with others.
        I know inside when I've done
            something wrong.

Even though I walk through the darkest valley, I fear no evil; for you are with me; your rod and your staff—they comfort me.
God is there in bad times as well as good times:
    when I'm in trouble;
    when I'm sick;
    when I'm afraid;
    when I don't know what to do.

You prepare a table before me in the presence of my enemies;
God wants me to get along with all people:
    people I don't like;
    people I don't trust;
    people I don't even know.

you anoint my head with oil; my cup overflows.
God makes me feel special.
    And I am special.
    I am a child of God.
    God loves me just the way I am.

Surely goodness and mercy shall follow me all the days of my life, and I shall dwell in the house of the LORD my whole life long.
When I think about God,
    I am happy
    Because I know
    God will always love me.

Supplies

Reproducible 8B, scissors, crayons or felt-tip markers, pennies or metal washers, tray or cardboard, stapler and staples, scraps of paper, plastic drinking straws, masking tape

To the Rescue!

Make a copy of the baby birds **(Reproducible 8B)** for each child in the class. Show the children how to assemble the birds with the loop of paper at the top. If you have an extended class time, let the children color the birds however they wish.

Make sure there are several birds for each child. Tape a penny or a metal washer to the base of each bird. Place all the birds on a tray or a piece of cardboard. Make the plastic drinking straw hooks by bending down the top three inches of the straw and taping as shown in the illustration. If you have accordion-necked straws, simply bend the straws into position.

Say: Psalm 23 reminds us of how God cares for the people as a shepherd cares for sheep. God provides food for us. God gives us a time of rest. God leads us in right paths so that we don't get lost. God is with us in bad time and good times. God rejoices with us and is sad when we are sad. God is always there. God treats us with gentleness. Whenever I think about caring for someone or something with gentleness, I always think about baby animals, particularly birds.

Ask: Have you ever seen a newly hatched baby bird? What is it like? Is it able to care for itself? What would happen if a fierce wind came up and all the baby birds were blown out of the nest?

Say: Let's see what kind of bird parents you would be. A big storm has blown through during the night. The wind was fierce and broke apart the tiny little bird nest. Baby birds are scattered all over the place.

Scatter the baby birds all over the room. Then give each child the drinking straw hook. The children must hook each baby bird with the straw and bring it back to the nest. The only catch is that the children have to hold the straws in their teeth. When all the birds have been returned to their nest (the tray or cardboard), cheer.

Ask: What did you have to do to get the baby birds back to the nest?
(You had to be gentle or they would blow off the hook.)

Say: God loves us and cares about us. God gently tries to help us find the right way so that we do not get lost. God wants us to be just as gentle and considerate as we help others. Sometimes people think it is cool to be mean and rough with other people. But that's not the way God wants us to be.

We can treat others with gentleness.

86

No Wimps Allowed!

Have the children stand up and form a circle.

Say: **Being gentle does not mean being either a weak person or a pushover. Sometimes being gentle means you also have to be strong. You must put the needs of other persons ahead of your own. As we pass the birds, I'm going to clap my hands. Then, I will stop clapping. If you are holding a bird, you must tell of some way you can be considerate of others this week. Then the whole class will respond with the Bible verse: "Let your gentleness be known to everyone" (Philippians 4:5).**

Start and stop clapping often enough to keep the game going quickly. When the children begin to get bored, bring them to the worship area.

Supplies

paper birds from "To the Rescue" activity (Reproducible 8B)

Fruit Basket Prayers

Have the children stand in a circle. Hold a piece of plastic fruit.

Ask: **What fruit of the Spirit word did we learn today?** (*Invite the children to guess. Accept "gentle" or "gentleness."*) **What does it mean to be gentle?** (*Invite the children to share.*)

Say: **When we are gentle we are kind and considerate of others. We are not harsh or unfriendly.**

Ask: **What would a gentle reminder be? a gentle touch? a gentle rain? a gentle woman or man? a gentle scolding?**

Say: **When the Holy Spirit lives in you, you want to live a life of gentleness toward others.**

Supplies

plastic fruit

 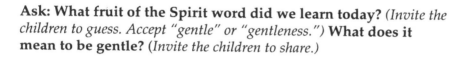
We can treat others with gentleness.

Pray: **Dear God, thank you for showing gentleness toward us. Amen.**

Toss the plastic fruit to one of the children in the circle.

Pray: **Dear God, we thank you for (***Child's name***). Help (***him or her***) be gentle and considerate of others. Amen.**

Then have the child toss the plastic fruit to another child. Pray for that child. Continue tossing the fruit around the circle until everyone has had a turn.

Let your gentleness be known to everyone. (Philippians 4:5)

Jesus teaches us that it is good to be gentle. There are many items in this picture that make us think of gentleness. Can you find them?
4 butterflies, 2 caterpillars, a baby lamb, a nest with baby birds, 3 rabbits, 2 frogs, 3 mice, 2 turtles, 2 ladybugs, a cloud, and 10 flowers.

REPRODUCIBLE 8A

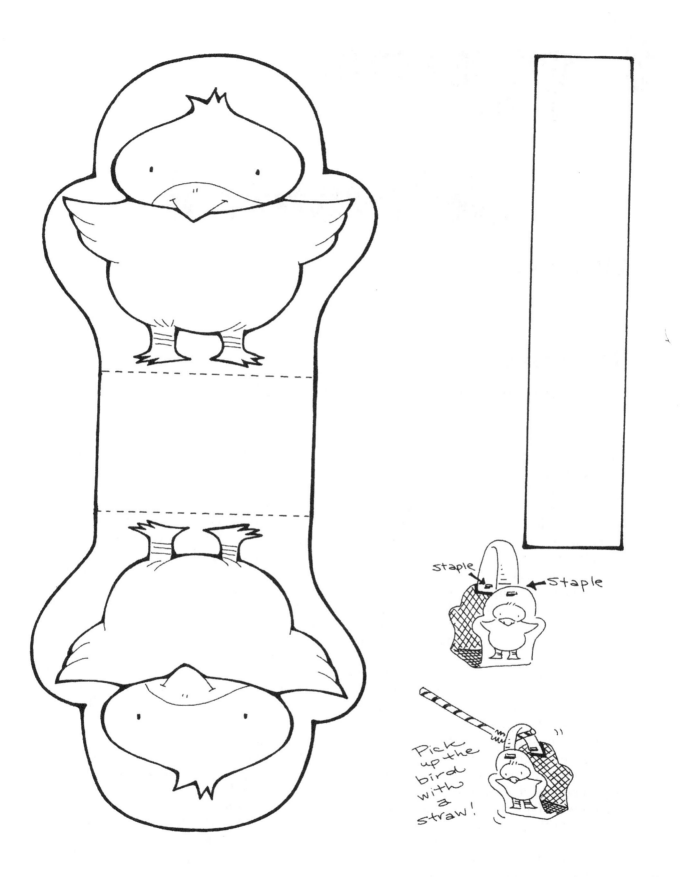

staple ← Staple

Pick up the bird with a straw!

Fruit of the Spirit - Elementary

Self-control

Bible Verse

Let us choose what is right.

Job 34:4

Bible Story

Galatians: 5:22–23; Daniel 1:1–20

The story of young Daniel is a good example of self-control. The setting for the first chapter of the Book of Daniel is the capture of Jerusalem by King Nebuchadnezzar. The Babylonians took captive a young man by the name of Daniel, whose name means "God is my judge." It appears to have been a custom for some of the young men to have been selected for higher education. This was evidently a great honor and required great mental and physical stamina. These young courtiers would be trained to serve the king.

Daniel and his friends were selected for this type of training. Eating rich foods and wines from the king's table was one of the privileges of this position. Since this was enjoyable, it must have been tempting for the young men to give in to this custom. However, Daniel and his companions exhibited large amounts of self-control. Daniel and his friends were faithful to God, and they refused to disobey the dietary laws of God. Since they had no control over how the food was prepared, the young men insisted on eating only vegetables, because that was the

only way they could be sure that they were obeying God's dietary laws.

The steward who was in charge of the well-being of these young men was concerned that he would be blamed for any ill health they might suffer. Even the king was angry that the men would turn down the food served at his own table. However, Daniel managed to convince both that they should be allowed to put this to a test. How surprised both the king and the steward were when Daniel and his friends ended up healthier and stronger than those who ate the richer foods. The king came to admire Daniel and his friends for their self-control.

Learning to make wise choices is one of the skills of growing up. Learning to choose what is right is an issue of self-control. Children do not have many autonomous choices allowed them. But they need to practice whenever possible so that when the time comes to make larger, more life-affecting choices, they are equipped to evaluate and choose wisely.

We can use self-control to help us make right choices.

If time is limited, we recommend those activities that are noted in **boldface**. Depending on your time and the number of children, you may be able to include more activities.

ACTIVITY	TIME	SUPPLIES	
Vegetable Soup	**5 minutes**	**Reproducible 9A; pencils, crayons, or felt-tip markers**	JOIN THE FUN
Scattered Categories	10 minutes	Reproducible 9B, scissors	
Temptations	10 minutes	Reproducible 9B, scissors, basket or bowl	BIBLE STORY FUN
Bible Story: Good Choice!	**10 minutes**	**None**	
Resist and Batik!	15 minutes	drawing paper, chalk, crayons, black tempera paint, cotton balls, small shallow bowl, plastic sandwich bags, newspaper, gum erasers	
Signs of Self-Control	5 minutes	None	LIVE THE FUN
Fruit Basket Prayers	**5 minutes**	**plastic fruit**	

Fruit of the Spirit - Elementary

Vegetable Soup

Make a copy of the scrambled word puzzle **(Reproducible 9A)** for each child. The picture above each word will give a clue to the word. If you have first-graders, let them work with older children if spelling is difficult. Or write the unscrambled words on a piece of paper.

Greet the children as they arrive. Have the materials set out for them. If you have an extended arrival time let the children color the pictures as well.

Ask: What's your favorite vegetable? Is it one of these pictured here? Why do you like it? How does your family prepare it?

Say: Today's Bible story talks about some young men who have an opportunity to eat whatever they want, and yet they choose to eat healthy foods instead. They can use self-control to make right choices.

> **We can use self-control to help us make right choices.**

Scattered Categories

Divide the children into teams of three or four children per team. Give each team a food sheet **(Reproducible 9B)**. Have them cut apart the pictures of the various foods and spread them out on the table.

Say: Here are sixteen pictures of foods. Of these foods there are five categories. Each food will fit into one of these categories. Let's see if you can group them. Everyone on your table must agree with the choices. When you are finished shout, "Fruit of the Spirit!"

The categories are: Breads (bread, cereal, oatmeal muffin); Fruits (apple, banana, strawberry); Dairy (milk, yogurt, cheese); Meat (fish, chicken, eggs); Other Stuff (pie, cake, candy, ice cream). If the children have not managed to group the foods correctly after a few attempts, give them the correct categories.

Ask: Are there any foods you were unsure of? Why do you think pie, cake, candy, and ice cream are listed in a category called "Other Stuff"? *(These foods do not have much nutritional value and do not help to build healthy bodies. They are mostly sugar and fat.)*

Temptations

Supplies

Reproducible 9B, scissors, basket or bowl

Photocopy and cut out the food squares (**Reproducible 9B**). Place the pictures in a basket or bowl. Bring the children together in a circle with their chairs.

Say: Today's Bible lesson is on self-control. Daniel, a young man who is taken against his will from his homeland, has to have great self-control in our story in order to be faithful to God. The temptations that Daniel faces in this story are not unlike some of the same ones we face every day. We have to have great self-control so that we can choose to do what's right.

Select one child to be "IT." Remove IT's chair from the circle.

Say: In order for IT to join the circle, he or she must get rid of all the food in the basket or bowl. In order to do this, IT is going to come around to each of you and offer you a food picture. The person being offered the food must use great self-control, and say "No thank you, I'm not hungry." Even your neighbors will try to encourage you to take a square of food, saying things like, "Come on, you know you want it. Go ahead. Who will know?" But the person being offered the food is to respond by saying only: "No thank you, I'm not hungry." Let's have everyone practice that phrase.

Say it together several times until the children are familiar enough with it that they won't need prompting.

Say: Then IT will have to move on to another person in the circle. However, if you smile or grin or laugh in any way, then you have to take one of the food pictures. When all of the food pictures are gone, the game is over and the last person to get a food square will become the next IT.

Play until there have been several children in the role of IT or until the children get bored.

Say: Resisting temptation is never easy. People all around you are always trying to get you to do things you know you shouldn't do. And sometimes the things you want are not especially good for you. So you have to use your self-control to choose what is right.

We can use self-control to help us make right choices.

Good Choice!

by LeeDell Stickler

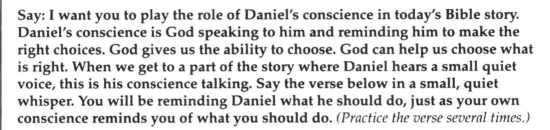

Say: I want you to play the role of Daniel's conscience in today's Bible story. Daniel's conscience is God speaking to him and reminding him to make the right choices. God gives us the ability to choose. God can help us choose what is right. When we get to a part of the story where Daniel hears a small quiet voice, this is his conscience talking. Say the verse below in a small, quiet whisper. You will be reminding Daniel what he should do, just as your own conscience reminds you of what you should do. *(Practice the verse several times.)*

Conscience Verse:
Choices, choices, everywhere
They'll put you to the test.
But if you use your self-control
Then you will choose what's best.

A long time ago in the land of Judah a great army swept across the land. It tore down the walls around the cities; it trampled the fields; it burned the Temple; and it carried off many of the people to become slaves in a new land.

Among those people who were forced to move away was a young man named Daniel. Daniel was very bright. He was very strong. He was very faithful to God. He worried about what would happen when he was far away from the place where he worshiped God. But then Daniel heard a small voice inside him speaking:

Conscience Verse

One day the king's steward came to where Daniel and other young men were working. "The king has sent me to pick the strongest and the smartest from among you. You will go to the palace and be personal servants of the king." The steward carefully looked over the group of young men. He chose Daniel and his friends Shadrach, Meshach, and Abednego as part of the group.

Daniel thought to himself, "This is good. I will get to live in the king's palace. I will be taught by the king's teachers." And a small voice inside him said:

Conscience Verse

ALL-IN-ONE BIBLE FUN

On the first day the steward brought the young men trays and trays of food, right from the king's table. There were pastries and meats and fruits. There were foods that Daniel and his friends had never seen before. Daniel knew his group was in trouble. Inside he heard a small quiet voice:

Conscience Verse

"This food looks wonderful," said Daniel to the steward, "but we cannot eat it. My friends and I follow God's laws. Our laws forbid that we eat such foods."

"But, but, you can't refuse the king's food!" the steward stammered. "What if you become ill? I will be blamed! I will get into trouble."

Daniel didn't want to get the steward into trouble. Then he heard a small voice inside him speaking:

Conscience Verse

Daniel had a thought. "Test us for ten days. Let us eat only fresh vegetables and water. Then compare us to those who ate the king's food."

The steward agreed, even though he didn't want to. He couldn't force the young men to eat, after all. So, for ten days he brought Daniel and his friends only fresh vegetables to eat and water to drink. Then the ten days came to an end.

The steward inspected all the young men. Daniel and his friends looked healthy and fit. Daniel and his friends were even stronger and faster than those who had been eating the king's food. And besides, Daniel and his friends showed that they had learned more and were wiser than any of the other young men.

"You have convinced me," said the steward. "From now on healthy food is what you will be given." Daniel smiled to himself as the small voice inside him said:

Conscience Verse

And when the three years of training was over, Daniel and his friends were by far the strongest, the smartest, and the wisest in all of the kingdom.

Conscience Verse

Say: When Daniel choose to eat good food, his choice was about more than just choosing food. It was about choosing to be obedient to God.

Supplies

drawing paper, chalk, crayons, black tempera paint, cotton balls, small shallow bowls, plastic sandwich bags, newspaper, gum erasers

Resist and Batik!

Batik is a way of making designs on cloth with wax and dye. Wax is used on the cloth to resist (repel) the colored dye. Have the children use a simpler process to make a painting on paper that will resemble the traditional batik.

As they work remind the children that Daniel used his self-control to resist the temptation to eat the king's food. God also calls upon us to use our self-control to resist doing things we shouldn't do.

Cover the tables with newspaper. Give each child a piece of drawing paper.

Say: I'll bet it was hard for Daniel and his friends to resist all that good food from the king's table and eat only fresh vegetables and water. But Daniel knew that the food laws of his faith were important. If he disobeyed those, he was disobeying God. So Daniel resisted the temptation to eat those foods. He used his self-control to resist.

Have each child draw a picture of her or his favorite fruits or vegetables on the drawing paper with colored chalk. Use thick chalk lines. Make the shapes of the objects large and simple.

Then let the children color inside the chalk lines with crayons. They can use any color except black. Instruct the children not to color over the chalk lines and leave spaces between the colored parts.

Encourage each child to write the Bible verse for today with a bright crayon. ("Let us choose what is right" Job 34:4) Then have each child use a gum eraser to gently wipe away the chalk lines.

Pour the black tempera paint into a shallow dish. Have the children slip their hands into plastic sandwich bags. Dip the cotton balls lightly in the black tempera paint and pass them gently over the paintings. Don't overlap. The crayon areas will resist the tempera paint.

Have the children turn the plastic sandwich bags inside-out with the cotton balls inside. (Hands should still be clean.) Set aside the Bible verse posters until they are dry.

> We can use self-control to help us make right choices.

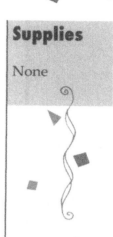

Signs of Self-control

Bring the children to the worship area.

Say: Having self-control is not easy. We need God's help so that we make the right choices.

Teach the children signs from American Sign Language for the abbreviated Bible verse.

Choose: thumb and forefinger of the right hand pretend to pick something from the left-hand "V."
What: Draw the tip of the right index finger downward across the left open palm.
Is: Hold the pinky finger up and move hand forward and backward.
Right: Place the little finger edge of the right "G" hand on top of the index finger of the left "G" hand so that both index fingers point forward, one above the other.

Have the children listen to the statements printed below and then sign this verse.

Say: Whenever we are tempted to disobey our parents: (*Sign the verse.*)
When the urge to play overcomes the urge to do homework: (*Sign the verse.*) **When we want to bend the rules so that we can win once in a while:** (*Sign the verse.*) **When we know that whining will get our parents to give in and get us what we want:** (*Sign the verse.*)

Fruit Basket Prayers

Have the children stand in a circle. Hold a piece of plastic fruit. Toss the plastic fruit to one of the children in the circle.

Pray: Dear God, we thank you for (*child's name***). Help (***him or her***) use self-control and make right choices. Amen.**

Then have the child toss the plastic fruit to another child. Pray for that child. Continue tossing the fruit around the circle until everyone has had a turn.

97

Vegetable Soup

What goes into Daniel's soup?
Unscramble the words to find out.

amfoot

nocr

apes

nabes

babaceg

tebes

inoon

aroctrs

topaot

eeppprs

hquass

REPRODUCIBLE 9A

ALL-IN-ONE BIBLE FUN

bread

milk

eggs

banana

cereal

apple

yogurt

cheese

chicken

fish

strawberry

oatmeal muffin

pie

cake

ice cream

candy

Honesty

Bible Verse

Be honest and you show that you have reverence for the LORD.

Proverbs 14:2, GNT

Bible Story

Luke 19:1–10

The story of Zacchaeus is found only in the Book of Luke. Zacchaeus was the chief tax collector in Jericho. It seems that Zacchaeus had amassed a fortune in dishonest revenue from his tax-collecting practices. A tax collector was required to collect a set amount of tax for Rome. Anything else the tax collector acquired he could keep.

We do not know whether or not Zacchaeus' conscience bothered him. What we do know is that he heard about Jesus and really wanted to see him. However, Zacchaeus was a very short man and could not see over the crowds; so, he climbed a tree alongside the road. From there he not only saw Jesus, but Jesus saw him. Though his was an unpopular decision, Jesus went with Zacchaeus to spend some time in his home.

Jesus had a profound effect on the life of Zacchaeus. We are not told whether Jesus lectured Zacchaeus. We are told that

Zacchaeus changed. He did not give up his job as a tax collector, but he did change his business practices. He divided his possessions and gave half to the poor. He repaid those he defrauded four times what he had taken from them.

One can only assume that by having placed the blame for his dishonesty squarely upon himself and taking on a great penalty for his wrongs, Zacchaeus turned his life into that of an honest man. Jesus blessed Zacchaeus and his newfound honesty. This honesty was rewarded by Zacchaeus truly finding God.

When asked in a survey to identify the top ten virtues that parents and Sunday school teachers want children to acquire, honesty was the top one on everyone's list. Let's help children learn that they should not take what belongs to someone else, lie, or cheat. These are important lessons for children to learn and will stick with them for life.

Be honest.

If time is limited, we recommend those activities that are noted in **boldface**. Depending on your time and the number of children, you may be able to include more activities.

ACTIVITY	TIME	SUPPLIES	
Catch the Thief!	**10 minutes**	**Reproducible 10A, poster-board, crayons or pencils, plastic sandwich bags, cookies or crackers, platter, paper napkins, plastic or real coins**	JOIN THE FUN
Cops and Robbers	10 minutes	plastic or real coins, crayons, bag	JOIN THE FUN
Play Gotcha!	10 minutes	Reproducible 10B, masking tape, crayons or felt-tip markers, plastic or real coins	BIBLE STORY FUN
Bible Story: Jesus and the Tax Collector	**10 minutes**	**None**	BIBLE STORY FUN
Downright Upright!	10 minutes	plastic or real coins	BIBLE STORY FUN
Honest to Goodness	5 minutes	None	LIVE THE FUN
Honest Prayers	**5 minutes**	**None**	LIVE THE FUN

JOIN THE FUN

Supplies

Reproducible 10A, poster-board, crayons or pencils, plastic sandwich bags, cookies or crackers, platter, paper napkins, plastic or real coins

Catch the Thief!

Make a copy of the maze (**Reproducible 10A**) for each child. Move all the chairs to one side of the room so that the children will have to pay to get a chair to sit in. Some children may choose to work on the floor. They'll be charged a floor tax. As each child comes into the room, give them sandwich bags with ten coins and a copy of the maze. Make a poster that will indicate what the children will have to pay in order to use one of the following items: chair/2 coins; floor/2 coins; crayon/3 coins; table/3 coins; cookie/2 coins.

Say: Today we are going to talk about a Bible character you may know. His name was Zacchaeus and he was a tax collector. He was also a thief because he collected more money than the people really needed to pay. The people disliked him because he became wealthy by cheating them. We are going to experience some of what the people might have felt as we work today. I am going to be Zacchaeus. You are the people of Jericho. In order to work today you will be charged a "use" tax on all the equipment.

A child paying the required amount for each of the items will still have enough to purchase a cookie. But as Zacchaeus you will cheat the children and charge more than the going rate. If the children protest, shrug your shoulders and say, "What can I do? It's the Romans. Blame them, not me!"

Be honest.

Supplies

plastic or real coins, crayons, bag

Cops and Robbers

Place the coins in a bag. Have the children stand in a circle with their hands held behind their backs. Walk around the circle and place either a coin, a crayon, or nothing in their hands. Caution the children as soon as their hands are touched, they must close their fingers so that no one will know what they have. Those who have a coin are the robbers; those who have the crayons are the cops (for writing tickets); and those that have nothing are the citizens. The object is to form a team with one of each of the three characters on it.

The children will go around to one another and ask for one of the other three. For example, a cop will ask, "Are you a robber?" If the person is a robber she or he will link arms and they will try to find a citizen. When a team of three is complete they will go to the storytelling area and sit together to wait for the other teams.

Play Gotcha!

Give each team of three a Gotcha gameboard **(Reproducible 10B)** and twenty-five coins. On one side of one coin in each set of twenty-five coins, place a piece of masking tape. This becomes the "Gotcha!" coin. Have the children place all the coins on the table. Make sure the coin with the masking tape is face-down. Mix the coins up by scooting them around and around. Be careful not to accidentally turn up any of the coins.

Ask: Is it okay to take something that doesn't belong to you? *(no)* **Is it okay to cheat someone?** *(no)* **Is it okay to take more than your fair share?** *(no)* **Is it okay to tell a lie?** *(no)*

Say: We're going to play a game called "Gotcha!" Everyone knows it is wrong to steal, or to take what does not belong to you. Many times people don't pay attention to this because they think they will never get caught. In this game someone will get caught.

Continue: The first thing you will do is to mix up the coins so you don't know which one has the piece of tape on the back. Then place each coin on a circle on the Gotcha gameboard. Don't look underneath or it will spoil the game.

Continue: Decide who is going to go first, second, and third. The first player will choose a coin from the board. Turn it over. If it doesn't have a piece of tape on the back, that player may keep the coin. The turn will pass to the second player who does the same thing. Then the turn will pass to the third player and so forth.

Continue: Each time a player picks up a coin, turns it over, and keeps it, the game will begin again. When a player turns up the "Gotcha!" coin, that means he or she has been caught stealing. That player must give back all of the coins he or she has collected. The others get a point for each coin they have collected.

Continue: Then mix the coins up, and start the game again. When time is up we will add up the points.

Play until the children begin to get bored with the activity. Remind the children that they are playing a game to point out that people who steal always get caught, eventually.

Be honest.

Jesus and the Tax Collector

by LeeDell Stickler

> Invite the children to be a part of the telling of the Bible story today. There is a repeated verse that Zacchaeus speaks. Encourage the children to say it with you after the first time. Note the changes on the last repetition.

Once in the city of Jericho there lived a man named Zacchaeus. He was a tax collector for the Romans. Now, no one liked paying taxes to the Romans anyway, but Zacchaeus made it even worse. He took not only the required tax money, but he also took a little extra. The extra money he kept for himself. Zacchaeus was a wealthy man.

"No wonder he is so rich," the people said. "No wonder we are so poor." When Zacchaeus would pass by, the people looked away.

And Zacchaeus would say:
It's my job to take the taxes
(though I take more than is due).
If people hate me 'cause I'm rich,
Just what am I to do?

One day word spread quickly through the marketplace of Jericho. "Jesus is coming! Jesus is coming!" Everyone in the town wanted to see this man. They had heard stories of how Jesus had caused the lame to walk and the blind to see.

Zacchaeus wanted to see Jesus too. He had heard the stories. But mostly he wanted to meet the man who said that being wealthy in God's kingdom isn't important. "That will be the day!" Zacchaeus said to himself.

And Zacchaeus would say:
It's my job to take the taxes
(though I take more than is due).
If people hate me 'cause I'm rich,
Just what am I to do?

So Zacchaeus closed his tax booth and made his way to the road where Jesus would pass. Already a crowd had begun to gather. There wasn't a space for Zacchaeus, who was a very short man.

Zacchaeus stood on his tiptoes, but he could not see over the peo-

ALL-IN-ONE BIBLE FUN

ple. He tried to look between them, but the people wouldn't budge.

"Go away, you little man! Why should we make space for you?" And the people would crowd together, making sure Zacchaeus couldn't see the road.

**And Zacchaeus would say:
It's my job to take the taxes
(though I take more than is due).
If people hate me 'cause I'm rich,
Just what am I to do?**

Many tall trees grew close to the side of the road. Zacchaeus had an idea. He ran to the nearest tree and began to climb. "Now," thought Zacchaeus, "I will be able to see Jesus when he comes down the road."

Zacchaeus had just gotten settled when he spotted Jesus and his friends. The crowd grew quiet as Jesus stopped beneath the tree where Zacchaeus was sitting. Jesus looked up. He looked right at Zacchaeus. "Zacchaeus! Come down out of that tree right now!"

The crowd gasped. Jesus was talking to Zacchaeus! No one in the town talked to Zacchaeus!

"Zacchaeus, today I'm coming to your house," Jesus announced.

Zacchaeus was stunned. Then he shimmied down the tree and hurried home. He couldn't believe it. Jesus was coming to his house! To his house! Jesus would be the most important visitor he had ever had.

As he prepared for Jesus' visit, Zacchaeus began to think. He thought about all the money he had taken from the people of the town. Then Zacchaeus knew he had to make some changes.

**And Zacchaeus said to himself:
It's my job to take the taxes
(though I take more than is due).
If people hate me 'cause I'm rich,
Just what am I to do?**

That evening, Zacchaeus told Jesus, "You know what kind of a person I am and yet you still choose to eat with me. I know I need to make changes in my life. So, I've decided to give half of my belongings away. And all the money I have taken, I will give back—four times as much."

**And then Zacchaeus said:
My job is taking taxes
(I'll only take what's due.)
For Jesus came into my life,
And showed me what to do.**

Supplies

plastic or real
coins

Downright Upright!

Ask: In today's Bible story what did Zacchaeus do that was dishonest? *(He took more tax money than was required.)* **Is it dishonest to collect taxes?** *(No, but it is dishonest to take more than the prescribed amount.)* **What did Zacchaeus do to make amends?** *(He gave half of his possessions to the poor and returned more than four times the money he had stolen.)*

Say: Zacchaeus was a thief. But when Jesus came into his life Zacchaeus decided to change his ways. Jesus knew that God sent him into the world to find those people who were doing wrong and bring them back to the right path.

Have the children form a circle with their hands behind their backs. Select one child to be "IT."

Say: Jesus could look into Zacchaeus' heart. Jesus knew that Zacchaeus had done wrong but that he basically wasn't a bad person; he was just a man who had strayed from the right path. Sometimes we can tell when someone isn't telling the truth.

I am going to go around the circle and place "stolen" coins in your hands—some of you, that is. *(To make the process a little easier, identify how many coins you are going to pass out.)*

IT will go around the circle and ask each of you, "Do you have my money?" Each person is to respond, "No, I'm downright upright!"

If IT thinks you have one of the stolen coins, then IT will tap you on the shoulder. Hold out your hands in front. If you have a coin, then you come to the center. If you don't, you stay where you are. IT can make three wrong guesses; then we'll start the game all over again.

Play until several of the children have an opportunity to be IT or until the children begin to get bored.

Ask: Was it easy or hard to see who was being honest when you were being IT? Was it easy or hard to be dishonest when you were in the circle?

Say: It's hard not to tell the truth, because we know how important it is to be honest. Even in a game, we know that being honest is important.

Be honest.

106

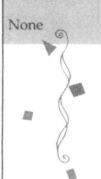

Honest to Goodness

Say: The Bible teaches us to be honest. In today's Bible story Zacchaeus was a dishonest man. He took money that did not belong to him. Zacchaeus was not doing good to others. But there is more to being honest than just not stealing. Being honest also means to tell the truth, to be fair, to mean what you say, and to be upright and trustworthy.

Ask: Can you think of a time when someone has not been honest with you? *(Invite the children to share events in their lives.)* What did you do when you found out? How did you feel about that person then?

Say: I am going to make a statement. If the person is being honest, say "Be honest!" If the person is not being honest, put your head in your hands and go "Oh, no!"

Use these statements:

1. Darryl cheated on his math test so he would get a passing grade. *(Oh, no!)*

2. Amy told her father that she was the one who broke the window. *(Be honest!)*

3. Elizabeth told her mother that her jacket was stolen when she really left it on the school bus. *(Oh, no!)*

4. When no one was looking Jeremy moved his game piece so he'd be closer to the finish. *(Oh, no!)*

5. When Melanie's best friend asked her if she liked her new backpack, Melanie answered, "It's so like you. You really like those colors!" Even though Melanie didn't personally like the colors herself. *(Be honest!)*

6. Kyle admitted that he forgot to walk the dog and offered to clean up the mess in the kitchen. *(Be honest!)*

Honest Prayers

Bring the children together in a prayer circle.

Pray: Dear God, help us always to be honest. When we are honest, we show other people that we love you. Amen.

Find the Stolen Coins

The tax collector has stolen money from people.
Can you find where he lives and return the money to the people?

Be honest and you show that you have reverence for the LORD.
Proverbs 14:2, GNT

REPRODUCIBLE 10A

ALL-IN-ONE BIBLE FUN

Gotcha Game!

All-in-One
BIBLE ELEMENTARY
FUN

Forgiveness

Bible Verse

You must forgive one another.

Colossians 3:13, GNT

Bible Story

Matthew 18:23–35

Jewish law in New Testament times stated that forgiving someone three times was sufficient. When Peter questioned Jesus about how often he should forgive someone, Peter himself suggested a generous seven times—more than twice the amount called for by law. However, for Jesus, even this is not enough. Jesus says we must forgive seventy-seven times, which means infinitely. God's forgiveness requires that our forgiveness of others be limitless.

Jesus illustrates his point by comparing the kingdom of heaven to a king who wished to be repaid a debt from his servant. The servant owed the king a substantial amount of money. The king, however, generously forgave the servant the entire debt.

Immediately following this the forgiven servant was asked to forgive a much smaller debt owed him by a fellow servant. However, this unforgiving servant refused to forgive the small debt owed to him by a

fellow servant, instead of exhibiting forgiveness and generosity. The unforgiving servant not only demanded payment of the debt owed him, but had his poor fellow servant thrown into prison. When the king learned of this callous behavior on the part of the servant he had forgiven, he rebuked the servant and then had him treated even more harshly than the unforgiving servant had treated his fellow servant.

Jesus wanted people to understand that if we expect God to forgive us, then we must offer forgiveness to one another.

Children are quick to forgive. They do not want to be estranged from any member of their immediate group. However, making the first step is sometimes difficult. Help the children practice asking for forgiveness. Model the words and the actions. Point out that asking for forgiveness also means attempting to change the behavior that caused the offense.

Forgive one another.

If time is limited, we recommend those activities that are noted in **boldface**. Depending on your time and the number of children, you may be able to include more activities.

ACTIVITY	TIME	SUPPLIES	
Color, Fold, Forgive	**10 minutes**	**Reproducible 11A, crayons or felt-tip markers, construction paper, scissors**	JOIN THE FUN
Please Forgive Me!	10 minutes	None	
To Infinity and Beyond	10 minutes	masking tape, 3 balls	BIBLE STORY FUN
Bible Story: The Unforgiving Servant	**10 minutes**	**chair, purple or royal blue cloth, paper crown, large book**	
BV Reminder	10 minutes	Reproducible 11B, business-size envelopes, white glue, crayons or felt-tip markers	
Whaddaya Gonna Do?	5 minutes	None	LIVE THE FUN
Crisscross Prayers	**5 minutes**	**None**	

111

Fruit of the Spirit - Elementary

Supplies

Reproducible 11A, crayons or felt-tip markers, construction paper, scissors

Color, Fold, Forgive

Make a copy of the storybook **(Reproducible 11A)** for each child in the group. Cut construction paper to the appropriate size to make covers for the book.

Greet the children as they come into the room. Give each child a storybook. Show the children how to cut out the storybook on the solid line and then fold and color the pages to make their books. Those who wish to do so can make covers from construction paper.

Say: This book is a shorter version of today's Bible story. It talks about forgiveness.

Ask: What do you do when you ask for forgiveness? *(You say you are sorry and promise not to repeat whatever it was that caused the offense.)*

> Forgive one another.

Supplies

None

Please Forgive Me!

Bring the children together in a circle with their chairs.

Say: Today's Bible lesson is about forgiveness. Each of us at some time or other has had the opportunity to tell someone we are sorry and be forgiven. It's a good feeling when someone says, "You're forgiven." Let's play a game.

Select one child to be "IT." Remove IT's chair from the circle. IT will kneel in front of each child in the group (in any order at all). IT will say in the most sincere voice possible, "Please forgive me!" The person will pat IT on the head, and then say, "I'm sorry but I just can't forgive you." However, if the person responding laughs, giggles, or smiles, this means he or she really has forgiven IT. That child must then change places with IT. IT may use his or her voice, facial expression, or body movement to make the person in the circle smile. The one thing IT cannot do is touch that person.

To Infinity and Beyond

Supplies

masking tape,
3 balls

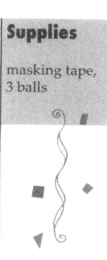

Divide the children into three teams. Give each team one ball. Use masking tape to make three squares of identical size on the floor. The ideal size would be twenty-four inches to a side. Place a line about six feet back from each square. Give each team its designation: A, B, or C.

Say: Here is your mission for today. Each team has a ball. The object of the game is for each team to roll the ball so that it stops somewhere inside the masking tape square. Each team must stand behind the masking tape line. Then each member of a team gets a designated number of tries. Each team will select one member to be the Counter. When the team has gotten three balls in the space, the Counter shouts, "To Infinity and Beyond!"

Continue: Each team member only gets one turn. At that team member's turn he or she can only throw the ball a certain number of times. I will tell you how many times. If the team still hasn't gotten three balls into the square after everyone has had a turn, the team must sit down.

Assign these designated rolls:

Each member of the "A" team can roll the ball three times from the starting line.

Each member of the "B" Team can roll the ball seven times from the starting line.

Each member of the "C" team can roll as often as they want until there are three balls in the square.

Play until one of the teams gets three balls into the square. Then call all the children together.

Ask: Which team had it the easiest? (*The team that could roll the ball as often as it wanted.*) **Which team had it the hardest?** (*The team that could only roll the ball three times.*)

Say: In Bible times there was a law that said a person only had to forgive another person three times. When Peter was talking to his friend Jesus, he suggested that they forgive seven times, more than twice as much. But Jesus had another idea altogether. Jesus said a person should forgive as often as it was called for. If after all God forgives us whenever we ask, then we should be willing to forgive others that often.

113

The Unforgiving Servant

by LeeDell Stickler

Say: Jesus often told stories to help the people understand what he was teaching. The people didn't understand when Jesus was teaching about forgiveness. So Jesus used this example to help them.

Make copies of the play. Select children to play the characters. You will need: the narrator, Jesus, Peter, the King, First Servant, Second Servant, Third Servant, and the guards. Place a chair in the center of the room. Cover it with royal blue or purple fabric. Make a crown from paper. Use a large book for the accounts book.

Narrator: One day Jesus and his friend Peter were talking about forgiveness. The law said that a person only had to forgive another person three times. Peter wondered if this were really enough.

Peter: If someone does something wrong to me, how many times should I forgive them? Is seven times enough?

Jesus: Seven times is not enough, Peter. You should forgive someone seventy-seven times.

Narrator: Jesus told this story to help them understand. Once there was a king who wanted to settle his accounts.

King: Bring me my account books. I wish to see who owes me money.

First Servant: Alrighty now! *(Servant #1 brings the King a large book.)*

King: Hmmm. *(turns pages in his accounts book)* Here is one of my servants who owes me a great deal of money. Bring him to me.

First Servant: Alrighty, now. *(First Servant leaves and comes back with the Second Servant.)*

King: You owe me a great deal of money. You have not repaid your loan. So, I am going to sell you, your wife, your children, and all your possessions.

Second Servant: *(throws himself at the King's feet)* Oh, please kind King! Give me more time to repay the loan. I promise I will pay you every cent that I owe you.

ALL-IN-ONE BIBLE FUN

King: There is no way that you can ever repay me all that money. But you truly seem sorry. So, I will forgive your debt. As of this moment, you no longer owe me any money. *(Closes the account book with a slam.)*

Second Servant: *(kisses the hand of the King over and over again.)* Thank you, thank you, thank you. I thank you. My wife thanks you. My children thank you.

Narrator: The servant runs from the throne room. As he does, he bumps into a fellow servant.

Second Servant: *(bumping into Third Servant)* Whoa there! Just a minute. It seems to me that you owe me money.

Third Servant: *(looking a little scared)* Just a little. I'll pay you on Tuesday.

Second Servant: *(grabbing the Third Servant and shaking him)* I want the money now! Right now!

Third Servant: But I don't have the money now. I told you, I will pay you on Tuesday.

Second Servant: Not good enough. Guards! *(Guards come.)* Take him away for nonpayment of debt.

Narrator: So the guards take the Third Servant and put him in prison for not paying his tiny little debt. But soon word of what had happened got around to the King.

First Servant: *(whispering in the King's ear)* And he had the man thrown into prison because he did not have the money to pay his debt.

King: Call the Second Servant to come here right now!

First Servant: Alrighty, now. *(First Servant leaves and comes back pulling the Second Servant by the ear.)*

Second Servant: Ow, ow, ow, ow! What's the matter?

King: You wicked servant! I forgave you all your debt because you asked me to. Shouldn't you have done the same for your fellow servant? Because you are so unforgiving, I have changed my mind. You will go to prison until you can repay me every cent.

Jesus: Peter, from this story I want you to learn that if you want God to forgive you, then you must also forgive your brothers and sisters from your heart, as many times as it takes.

BV Reminder

Supplies

Reproducible 11B, business-sized envelopes, white glue, crayons or felt-tip markers

Make a copy of the Bible Verse Reminder (**Reproducible 11B**) for each child.

Say: Sometimes it is easy to forgive. Sometimes it is hard to forgive. But if we expect God to forgive us for our wrongs, then we must forgive those who mistreat us.

Have the children lick the flaps on the envelopes and seal them. Then show the children how to fold the envelopes in half. Fold up one inch on either end to act as feet to hold the envelopes upright. *(See the illustration on the page.)*

Cut out the figures of the puppy. Glue the heads, the tails, and the paws onto the envelopes as shown in the directions to make an easel. Then cut out the Bible verse reminders. Place them on the easel and put the puppy dog paws over them, holding them in place.

Say: Place this reminder in your room at home or somewhere where you will always see it. It will remind you that just as God forgives you, you are expected to forgive others.

Forgive one another.

Whaddaya Gonna Do?

Supplies

None

Teach the children signs from American Sign Language for the Bible verse: "Forgive one another."

Say: The Old Testament law said that a person had to forgive another person three times. This was the law. But Jesus knew that this was not enough. Jesus knew that God forgives us many more times than that. If God can forgive us as many times as it takes, then we too have to forgive others.

Read each of these statements. Then have the children respond with the Sign Language.

1. When someone steps upon your toe, whaddaya gonna do?

2. When someone takes your place in line, whaddaya gonna do?

3. When someone says something mean about you, whaddaya gonna do?

4. When someone forgets to come to your house to play, whaddaya gonna do?

5. When someone breaks your favorite toy, whaddaya gonna do?

6. When your mom or dad accuses you of something you didn't do, whaddaya gonna do?

7. If your brother knocks over your cold glass of milk, spilling it all over you, whaddaya gonna do?

Crisscross Prayers

Supplies

None

Have the children form a crisscross prayer circle. (*Cross right hand over left hand and take the crossed right and left hands of the persons on either side of you.*)

Pray: Dear God, we know we make mistakes. When we ask you to forgive us we expect you will do so. Help us to extend this same forgiveness to our brothers and sisters in you. Amen.

117

When the king heard what the first servant had done, he was very angry. He had the servant arrested and put into prison until the debt was paid.

Remember: Forgive others as God for-gives you.

Once there was a king...

The Unforgiving Servant

One day he called together all persons who owed him money.

"Pay me or go to prison," he said.

One man could not pay. He begged the king. "Give me more time."

The king forgave the man his debt and sent him on his way. The man was so happy he danced for joy.

As he left, the man ran into a friend who owed him money.

"Pay up or go prison," the man said.

REPRODUCIBLE 11A

ALL-IN-ONE BIBLE FUN

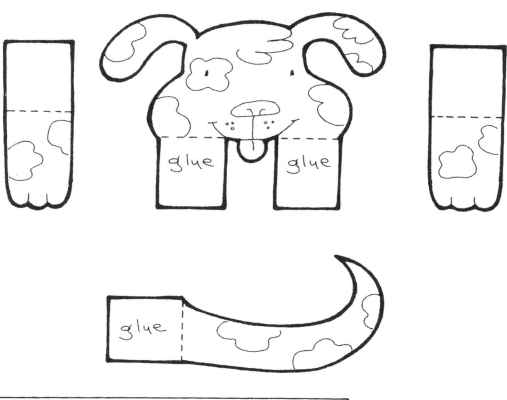

You
must
forgive
one
another.
(Colossians 3:13, GNT)

Glue head, paws, and tail to back of stand

Just as the Lord has forgiven you, so you also must forgive —

Glue on Bible Verse

All-in-One
BIBLE FUN
ELEMENTARY

Obedience

Bible Verse

For the love of God is this, that we obey God's commandments.

1 John 5:3, adapted

Bible Story

Matthew 24:45–51; Luke 12:41–48

Jesus often used familiar situations to help the people understand his complicated messages. Jesus explains the responsibilities of obedience to God in this passage from Matthew. Jesus uses the story of a faithful servant who has been placed in charge of his fellow servants while the master is away. Obedience to the master is of the utmost importance. How wonderful it is for the master to come home and find the servant doing just as he was told to do. Then Jesus tells about the foolish servant who sees that the master has been delayed, and takes advantage of the situation. Part of the story tells how the disobedient servant disobeys his master and mistreats the other servants. When the master returns early and discovers what has happened, that disobedient servant is severely punished.

In this Bible passage, Jesus is talking about the second coming and about the need for watchfulness and obedience. Humans do not know the exact time when God will come. Jesus cautions his disciples not to become complacent and lapse into bad habits. They must always be faithful. To be obedient to God only when we think that someone is watching is not enough. We must be obedient to the will of God at all times.

God calls us to live our lives as if God will show up at any moment. This obedience is not a call to just a set of rules and regulations, but to the heart and spirit of the Gospel, to loving God, and therefore caring for those whom God loves.

Children are often coerced into doing things because "no one will know" or "no one is looking." Being "caught" is not the point. If children know what the right behavior is and choose to do otherwise, this is just as wrong as if someone were watching.

Obey God's commandments.

If time is limited, we recommend those activities that are noted in **boldface**. Depending on your time and the number of children, you may be able to include more activities.

ACTIVITY	TIME	SUPPLIES
God's Top Ten	**10 minutes**	**Reproducible 12A, pencils**
Catch Them Being Good	10 minutes	construction paper, crayons or markers, scissors, tape
Sneaky Snitch	10 minutes	paper plate, items from the room that can be hidden in a child's hand such as crayons or erasers
Snatch It	10 minutes	masking tape, paper, scissors
Bible Story: Wise or Foolish?	**10 minutes**	**None**
Commandment Cut-Ups	10 minutes	Reproducibles 12A and 12B, scissors, envelopes
Commandment Put-Ups	5 minutes	Reproducible 12B, construction paper, glue
Rhythmic Repetition	5 minutes	Reproducible 12B
Pray and Obey	**5 minutes**	**None**

JOIN THE FUN

BIBLE STORY FUN

LIVE THE FUN

Reproducible 12A, pencils

God's Top Ten

Make a copy of the Ten Commandments puzzle **(Reproducible 12A)** for each child. One vowel is missing from the words in the puzzle. *(O)* When the children figure it out and fill in the missing spaces, then the commandments will be complete.

Say: **Today's Bible story is about being obedient even when no one is looking. People in Bible times and people today were and are expected to be obedient to God's laws all the time.**

> Obey God's commandments.

construction paper, crayons or markers, scissors, tape

Catch Them Being Good

Say: **Today's Bible story is about being obedient even when no one is looking. You may feel that adults are on the lookout trying to catch you doing something that is wrong, but today I'm going to try to catch you doing something good. When I do, I'm going to give you a pat on the back.**

Give each child a piece of construction paper. Have the children work together to trace one another's hand on the paper. Have the children cut out their handprints.

Let the children decorate the handprints with crayons or markers. If you want each child to receive his or here own handprint later, have the children write their names on their prints. Collect the handprints.

Surprise your children with a special pat on the back for being good throughout today's lesson. When you see a child sharing, paying attention, helping someone else, cleaning up and so forth, give that child a compliment and tape his or her handprint on the child's back.

Praise children for specific good behavior. Let them know how much you appreciate them for being trustworthy and obedient without anyone standing over them.

Be sure to catch every child being good.

Sneaky Snitch

Have the children form a large circle. Place a chair in the center of the circle.

Say: We are going to hear in today's Bible story about a servant who did some things he wasn't supposed to do when he thought no one was looking. But his master caught him.

Select one child to be "IT." IT will sit in the chair and hold the paper plate. Place several items on the plate such as crayons or erasers.

Say: I want all of you to put your hands behind your backs. I will walk around the circle and touch someone's hand. Then I will say, "No one's looking." At that point IT will close his or her eyes. Then I will say "Sneaky Snitch." The person whose hand I touched will then creep up to the chair and IT and will take a crayon or eraser back to the circle. Everyone will continue to hold their hands behind their backs. IT will open his or her eyes and have three chances to find the person who did it. After three wrong guesses the person who is holding the item will be the new IT.

Snatch It

Cut a piece of paper into a long narrow strip.

Have the children move to the center of the room. Select one child to be "IT." The remainder of the children will line up on the opposite side of the room. Put a masking tape "X" on the floor to indicate where IT is supposed to stand.

Ask: Have you ever done something you weren't supposed to do knowing that you would never get caught? *(Invite the children to share experiences.)* **Was it the right thing to do?** *(no)* **Why not?** *(If it's the wrong thing to do it's still wrong whether anyone catches you or not.)*

Say: Let's play a game today where the object of the game is to not be caught doing something. In fact, if you are caught moving at all, you have to go back to the beginning. But in order to win the game you have to snatch the paper.

Tape the paper on IT so that the paper hangs down IT's back. Have all the children line up against the wall.

Say: The object of the game is to sneak up on IT and snatch the paper before she or he turns around and catches you moving. If IT catches you moving, you have to go back to the start.

The first person to snatch the paper takes over the job as IT and the game begins again. Play until everyone has a chance to be IT.

Supplies

paper plate, items from the room that can be hidden in a child's hand such as crayons or erasers

Supplies

masking tape, paper, scissors

123

Wise or Foolish?

by LeeDell Stickler

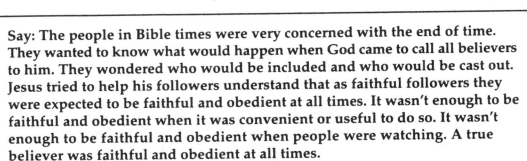

Say: The people in Bible times were very concerned with the end of time. They wanted to know what would happen when God came to call all believers to him. They wondered who would be included and who would be cast out. Jesus tried to help his followers understand that as faithful followers they were expected to be faithful and obedient at all times. It wasn't enough to be faithful and obedient when it was convenient or useful to do so. It wasn't enough to be faithful and obedient when people were watching. A true believer was faithful and obedient at all times.

Copy the lesson and select children to read and lead the parts of the servants and the masters.

Faithful Servant:
I am a faithful servant
as wise as wise can be.
I do just what my master says
Even when he cannot see.

I get up early in the mornings.
(Pantomime getting up, yawning, and jumping up.)
I hurry out to the fields to cut the grain. *(Pantomime swinging a scythe to cut the grain.)*
I serve food to my fellow servants. *(Pantomime serving food to others.)*
I pay them their wages on time. *(Pantomime paying the servants.)*
I watch over the sheep. *(Pantomime watching over the sheep.)*
I pick the grapes from the vine and see that they are pressed. *(Pantomime picking grapes and stomping on them.)*

I pick the olives from the tree and see that they are pressed into oil. *(Pantomime picking olives)*
I work very hard. *(Pantomime wiping sweat from your brow.)*

I am a faithful servant
as wise as wise can be.
I do just what my master says
Even when he cannot see.

Faithful Servant's Master:
I am the servant's master
My household's in his care.
I know that he is faithful
Even though I am not there.

He gets up early in the mornings.
(Pantomime getting up, yawning, and jumping up.)
He hurries out to the fields to cut the grain. *(Pantomime swinging a*

ALL-IN-ONE BIBLE FUN

scythe to cut the grain.)
He serves food to my fellow servants. (*Pantomime serving food to others.*)
He pays them their wages on time. (*Pantomime paying the servants.*)
He watches over the sheep. (*Pantomime watching over the sheep.*)
He picks the grapes from the vine and sees that they are pressed. (*Pantomime picking grapes* and *stomping on them.*)
He works very hard. (*Pats servant on the back.*)

Foolish Servant:
I am a foolish servant
so when my master goes away
I do just what I want to;
I don't waste a single day.

I sleep late in the morning. (*Pantomime sleeping and snoring.*)
Then I go out to the fields very slowly. (*Pantomime walking slowly.*)
I eat lots and lots of good food. (*Pantomime eating.*)
I drink wine until I can't stand up. (*Pantomime drinking and staggering.*)
I beat the other servants for not working hard enough. (*Pantomime beating the other servants.*)
I dance through the night. (*Pantomime dancing.*)
While my master is gone, I don't work very hard. (*Pantomime sitting down and fanning self.*)

Foolish Servant's Master:
I am the servant's master
My household's in his care.
I know that he is foolish
Whenever I'm not there.

He sleeps late in the morning. (*Pantomime sleeping and snoring.*)
He goes out to the fields very slowly. (*Pantomime walking slowly.*)
He eats lots and lots of food. (*Pantomime eating.*)
He drinks wine until he can't stand up. (*Pantomime drinking and staggering.*)
He beats the other servants for not working hard enough. (*Pantomime beating the other servants.*)
He dances through the night. (*Pantomime dancing.*)
He thinks that I don't know what he does. But I do. And boy, is he in trouble! (*Stands with fists on hips and looks down at the sitting Foolish Servant.*)

I am the servant's master
And he's in trouble deep.
He's neither wise nor faithful
and my rules he does not keep.
(*Master will take Foolish Servant by the ear and lead him off.*)

Supplies

Reproducibles 12A and 12B, scissors, envelopes

Commandment Cut-Ups

Make copies of the Commandment Cut-Ups **(Reproducible 12B)**. Cut each set of commandments into pieces, making sure to separate each commandment into two parts. Place the commandments in an envelope.

Please note that each commandment is also shown in a different typeface to help the children match the commandments. However, if the children are primarily nonreaders, this activity will be difficult.

Ask: In the story of the two servants, one was faithful at all times and one was faithful only when the master was around. Which one was the good servant? *(the first one)* **Why?** *(because he did what he was supposed to whether his master was watching or not)* **Why was the second servant the bad one?** *(because he only did what he was supposed to when the master was watching)* **Why did the second servant get into trouble?** *(He got caught.)* **What message do you think the disciples got from this story about being obedient to God?** *(that we should be faithful and obedient to God at all times, not just when someone is looking)*

Say: God gave us certain laws to live by. If we live by those laws, then we are being obedient to God.

Ask: What are these laws called? *(Ten Commandments)*

Review the commandments with the children from the "God's Top Ten" activity **(Reproducible 12A)**. Then divide the children into teams of three or four. Give each team an envelope with the Commandment Cut-Ups.

The object of the activity is for the children to put the two parts of each commandment together. When every commandment is assembled, have the team shout the Bible verse: "For the love of God is this, that we obey God's commandments" (1 John 5:3, adapted).

Supplies

Reproducible 12B, construction paper, glue

Commandment Put-Ups

Make copies of the Commandment Cut-Ups **(Reproducible 12B)** for each child.

Have the children glue the commandments onto a piece of construction paper.

Say: Put up your Ten Commandments somewhere in your house so that you will pass by them every day. Read them and think about them.

126

Rhythmic Repetition

Supplies

Reproducible
12B

Bring the children together in the worship center. Have them sit on the floor cross-legged.

Begin to clap out a rhythm as you say the Bible verse for today: "For the love of God is this, *(pause)* that we obey God's commandments." Continue repeating this until the children can say it with you. Then change the pattern.

Say: "For the love of God is this, that we love one another."

Have the children repeat the addition to the Bible verse in the same rhythm. Do this for five or six repetitions.

Say: "For the love of God is this. . . ."

Point to one of the children and let him or her fill in some action that will show that a person is faithful and obedient to God. Encourage the child to clap his or her hands and speak in the rhythm. Have the class repeat this action several times.

Say the beginning of the Bible verse again and point to a different child. Encourage children to clap their hands in a rhythmic fashion as they chant their additions to what it means to be faithful and obedient.

Continue until all of the children who wish to do so have had turns.

Then have the children say the Ten Commandments in unison, standing up and shouting out the number and then sitting down. For example, ONE *(Stand up, shout the number, sit down.)* "God is the only God." TWO *(Stand up, shout the number, sit down.)* "Worship only God." Continue all the way through the commandments. Use the Commandment Cut-up Sheet (**Reproducible 12B**) as a guide. The wording on the sheet is simple and may be more understandable to the children than the Exodus version.

Pray and Obey

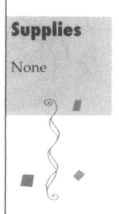

Supplies

None

Gather the children around in a prayer circle.

Pray: Dear God, we want to be obedient to you every day. Help us to follow your commandments. Amen.

God's Top Ten

One letter is missing. Can you discover what it is?

G__d is the __nly G__d.

W__rship __nly G__d.

D__n't use G__d's name
in a bad way.

Keep the Sabbath day h__ly.

H__n__r y__ur father
and m__ther.

D__ n__t c__mmit murder.

Be faithful t__
y__ur husband __r wife.

D__ n__t steal.

D__ n__t tell lies.

D__ n__t want what bel__ngs
t__ s__me__ne else.

REPRODUCIBLE 12A

ALL-IN-ONE BIBLE FUN

1. God is the only God.
2. Worship only God.
3. Do not use God's name in a bad way.
4. Keep the Sabbath day holy.
5. Honor your father and mother.
6. DO NOT COMMIT MURDER.
7. BE FAITHFUL TO YOUR HUSBAND OR WIFE.
8. Do not steal.
9. Do not tell lies.
10. Do not want what belongs to another.

Responsibility

Bible Verse

Let your light shine before others, so that they may see your good works.
Matthew 5:16

Bible Story

Galatians 5:22–23; Matthew 25:14–30

The parable of the three servants is a story of how we have been entrusted with the knowledge of God's Son Jesus. It is our responsibility to use whatever talents and gifts we have to further God's kingdom. Some of us have been given the ability to move people with the words we speak; others have been given the ability to cure the sick; and once in a great while we find that one of us has been given the ability to lead a nation closer to God.

Most of us have only seemingly small gifts to give to further God's kingdom, such as the ability to be a Sunday school teacher or collect money for the poor. But in the parable of the three servants we see that this does not absolve us of the responsibility of using those small gifts to bring the kingdom of God closer.

Perhaps the man with five thousand coins can be likened to a leader who has the ability to bring countries together to talk about peace. Perhaps the person with two thousand coins is like a local pastor with the ability to preach. These people have used their gifts to further God's kingdom. They have lived up to their responsibilities and increased their contributions.

Then perhaps the servant with the one thousand coins is like the average person. She or he may not ever shake up the world, and most people will hardly ever notice what this person does. This person will probably not even have an impact on an entire church congregation. But if the individual will use his or her gift to further the kingdom of God, then God's kingdom has increased.

Perhaps the Sunday school teacher will influence another leader, or the person who takes food to the poor will help feed a future pastor. We do not all have the same talents, but we all have the same responsibility. We have been entrusted with the news of Jesus, and it is up to us to spread the news.

We are responsible for telling others about Jesus.

If time is limited, we recommend those activities that are noted in **boldface**. Depending on your time and the number of children, you may be able to include more activities.

ACTIVITY	TIME	SUPPLIES
A Secret Message	**5 minutes**	**Reproducible 13A, pencils or crayons**
Fruity Fun	15 minutes	newspaper, paper plates, sponges, tempera paint, plastic sandwich bags, smocks, construction paper, felt-tip markers, large piece of paper
Room Zoom	5 minutes	masking tape, construction paper, felt-tip marker, crayon, glue stick or bottle, book, paintbrush, basket or box
Bible Story: The Parable of the Three Servants	**5 minutes**	**None**
Catch the Spirit	10 minutes	Reproducible 13B, crayons or felt-tip markers, scissors
Jump, Turn, Praise!	5 minutes	None
Let Your Light Shine	**5 minutes**	**None**

JOIN THE FUN

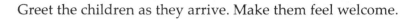

A Secret Message

Supplies

Reproducible 13A, pencils or crayons

Make a copy of A Secret Message **(Reproducible 13A)** for each child.

Greet the children as they arrive. Make them feel welcome.

Let the children discover the secret message in the puzzle.

Say: Today's lesson is about responsibility—our responsibility as Christians to tell the story of Jesus to other people. Each of us is blessed with fruit of the Spirit and it is our responsibility to spread the story of Jesus with the gifts we have been given.

Fruity Fun

Supplies

newspaper, paper plates, sponges, tempera paint, plastic sandwich bags, smocks, construction paper, felt-tip markers, large piece of paper

Cover the tables with newspaper. Place small amounts of tempera paint in the center of each paper plate. Copy Galatians 5:22–23 on a large piece of paper: "The fruit of the Spirit is love, joy, peace, patience, kindness, generosity, faithfulness, gentleness, and self-control."

Say: In the spring and summer it's fun to watch plants grow. First they get leaves, then they get flowers, and certain kinds of plants can also make fruits, such as apples, bananas, lemons, and grapes. All these fruits come from plants. If a plant has all the right things—air, water, good soil, and sunshine—its fruit is big and delicious. During these lessons we have been talking about certain qualities being the fruit of the Holy Spirit. The Holy Spirit is God's presence in us. When we have this, it causes us to produce fruit—not apples or oranges, but qualities that make us good people, such as love, joy, peace, patience, kindness, faithfulness, generosity, gentleness, and self-control. There are other fruits too, such as honesty, obedience, responsibility, and forgiveness. Our goal is to continue to produce these fruit of the Spirit as we grow as Christians.

Give each child a piece of construction paper. Have the children copy Galatians 5:22–23 onto their construction paper with felt-tip markers.

Have the children wear smocks. Let the children put their hands inside the plastic sandwich bags to hold the sponges. Dip the sponges in the tempera paint and press lightly several times on the poster. Do not mix the sponges and different colors of tempera paint unless you first wash the sponges and squeeze them out thoroughly.

When the children are finished painting, turn the sandwich bags inside-out and throw them away.

132

ALL-IN-ONE BIBLE FUN

Room Zoom

Set up at least six stations within the room. *(There should be half as many stations as there are children in the group.)* Each station will be designated by a piece of construction paper. Number each sheet of paper, but make sure the stations are not in sequential order. At the last station, set up a basket or box.

Place these items at Station One: a crayon, a felt-tip marker, a glue stick or bottle, a book, a paintbrush.

Write these words on six slips of paper: *hop, walk backwards, push with nose, run, baby-step, crawl, and tip-toe.*

Assign two children to each station. One will be the receiver; the other one will be the runner.

Say: Each of you is responsible for getting the items from Station One to Station Six (*or whatever is your last station***). You will move the items one at a time from station to station until they end up in the basket or box of the last station. Each team will draw a slip of paper to discover how they must move to get the items from station to station.**

Continue: For example, if Station One draws the crawl card, they will crawl to carry an item to the receiver at Station Two. If Station One draws the hop card, they will hop to carry the same item to Station Three. If Station Three draws the baby-step card, they will use baby-steps to move the item to Station Four and so on, until the item is moved to the last station.

Once the children understand what they are to do, let each team draw a travel slip that will indicate how the runner must deliver the item. When the last item is making the circuit, have every team cheer for the traveler at each station.

Play until the items have made the circuit.

Then say: Jesus gave his disciples a special message in Bible times. It was then their responsibility to spread the news of Jesus to everyone. Not every one of the disciples was an eloquent speaker. Not every disciple could heal. Not every disciple could teach. But each was expected to use his or her gifts to make sure that the gospel message went out.

Supplies

masking tape, construction paper, felt-tip marker, crayon, glue stick or bottle, book, paintbrush, basket or box

We are responsible for telling others about Jesus.

133

The Parable of the Three Servants

by LeeDell Stickler

Say: I want each of you to be a part of telling this story. In the story there are three servants. They are named Servant One, Servant Two, and Servant Three. These are very creative names, don't you think? I will refer to these servants during the telling of the story. I want you to come up with a body position that will represent each of the servants.

Divide the children into three groups. Group 1 will come up with the position for Servant One; Group 2 will decide on the position for Servant Two; and Group 3 will create the position for Servant Three. The individual groups will then teach the positions to the rest of the class. The children will then assume these positions when the section of the story says: "There was Servant One, Servant Two, and Servant Three." Notice at the very end that Servant Three was nowhere to be found.

Once there was a wealthy man. He was called away from his land for a time, but he didn't want to leave his property unsupervised. So he called together his three servants.

There was Servant One,
There was Servant Two,
And there was Servant Three.

He told his servants, "I am going away on a trip. I am leaving you in charge. I will give each of you according to your ability a certain amount of money. I expect you to be accountable when I return."

There was Servant One,
There was Servant Two,
And there was Servant Three.

To Servant One the master gave five thousand gold coins.

To Servant Two the master gave two thousand gold coins.

To Servant Three the master gave one thousand gold coins.

And then the master went on his way, leaving his three servants in charge of his money.

Servant One wisely invested his five thousand coins. Soon there were ten thousand coins.

The second servant wisely invested his two thousand coins. Soon there were four thousand coins.

But Servant Three had gotten only one thousand coins, and was afraid. So he went off and buried his coins in a hole in the ground.

There was Servant One,
There was Servant Two,
And there was Servant Three.

When the master came back, he called his servants to him.

There was Servant One,
There was Servant Two,
And there was Servant Three.

Servant One, who had received five thousand coins, gave his master those coins and then presented him with five thousand more.

"Well done, good and faithful servant," said the Master. '"You have been responsible over a small amount. So I will put you in charge of large amounts. Welcome to my house and share my happiness."

Servant Two, who had received two thousand coins, gave his master those coins and then presented him with two thousand more.

"Well done, good and faithful servant," said the Master. "You have been responsible over a small amount. So I will put you in charge of large amounts. Welcome to my house and share my happiness."

Servant Three, who had been given one thousand coins, gave the master the one thousand coins back and a good excuse.

"Oh, Master, I know you are a difficult man to work for. I was afraid. So I hid your money in the ground. Look! You have back exactly what you gave me." Servant Three handed over the one thousand coins.

"You bad and lazy servant!" shouted the Master. "At least you could have put my money in the bank and collected even a small amount of interest on it. Now, give me the coins I gave you and get out of my sight."

There was Servant One,
There was Servant Two,
And Servant Three was nowhere to be found.

135

Catch the Spirit

Make a copy of the Spirit Catchers **(Reproducible 13B)** for each child. Let the children color the pictures.

Say: Our Spirit Catcher can be a way of spreading the news about Jesus. Inside it are stories that can be found in the Bible telling about Jesus. You can use this Spirit Catcher to let people learn about the Jesus you know—the baby, the teacher, the healer, and the risen Christ.

When the children have finished coloring their Spirit Catchers, have them fold them in half along one dotted line. Then have them open up the Spirit Catchers and fold them in half along the other dotted line. These two folds will provide a center point.

Then turn the Spirit Catchers over, so that all the writing and drawings do not show. Take the corners and of each one and bring them to the center point. Crease along the dotted lines. Now all the pictures are showing on top.

Turn over the Spirit Catchers. Once again bring each corner of each one up to the center point. Crease along the dotted lines.

Turn over the Spirit Catchers so that only the pictures are showing. Fold in half so that on one side the pictures of the empty tomb and the healing hands are showing; on the other side are the baby Jesus and Jesus the teacher. Turn up the Spirit Catchers so that the loose edges are down.

Say: Put the thumb and index fingers of your left hands inside the pockets formed by the tomb and the baby on each Spirit Catcher. Put your thumbs and the index fingers of your right hands inside the pockets formed by the healing hands and Jesus the teacher.

Continue: While holding the Spirit Catchers, move your two index fingers together while moving your thumbs together. This will open the insides of the Catchers. Inside are words that tell about Jesus. If you lift up one of the flaps, the Bible references are listed that tell where the story can be found. Bring the points together. Then open the points in the opposite direction (index finger and thumb of each hand together). Inside those folds are other stories about Jesus.

Play a game where the children call out a number. Open and close the Spirit Catchers the required number of times. Then choose a story and have the children on the team look it up.

> We are responsible for telling others about Jesus.

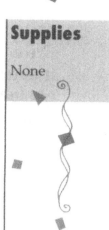

Jump, Turn, Praise!

Review the fruit of the Spirit with the song "Fruit of the Spirit Jump" to the tune of "Pick a Bale of Cotton." Encourage the children to pick a fruit of the Spirit or a Christian virtue and then make up a verse for it.

Fruit of the Spirit Jump

Gonna jump down, turn around
(Jump; turn around.)
Show my love and praise God.
(Cross arms over chest; raise arms.)
Jump down, turn around,
(Jump; turn around.)
Show my love and praise!
(Cross arms over chest; raise arms.)

Gonna jump down, turn around
(Jump; turn around.)
Show my joy and praise God.
(Pat hands on chest many times; raise arms.)
Jump down, turn around,
(Jump; turn around.)
Show my joy and praise!
(Pat hands on chest many times; raise arms.)

Gonna jump down, turn around
(Jump; turn around.)
Show my peace and praise God.
(Make a peace sign; raise arms.)
Jump down, turn around,
(Jump; turn around.)
Show my peace and praise!
(Make a peace sign; raise arms.)

Gonna jump down, turn around
(Jump; turn around.)
Be patient and praise God.
(Tap toes; raise arms.)
Jump down, turn around,
(Jump; turn around.)
Be patient and praise!
(Tap toes; raise arms.)

Supplies

None

Let Your Light Shine

Bring the children together in the storytelling area. Teach them the signs from American Sign Language for "Let your light shine."

Say: We are showing others that we are followers of Jesus whenever we do good things and whenever we help others. We are being responsible for spreading the good news of Jesus.

Go around the group and let each child think of something he or she can do in the coming week to spread the good news of Jesus. After each response let the class sign the verse. When everyone has shared then have them form a hand circle (all hands to the center) and say "Amen."

Supplies

None

137

Fruit of the Spirit - Elementary

A Secret Message

Cross out two letters, then circle one. When you get to an "X," circle the next letter. This means a new word is beginning. Repeat until you get to the end of the puzzle. Write the words in circles on the lines in order. What did Jesus tell us to do?

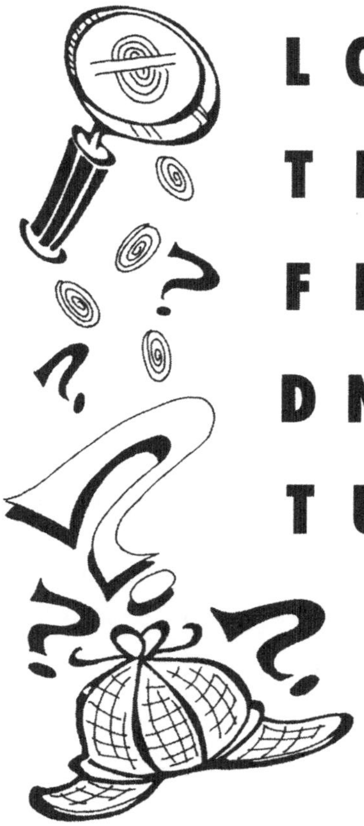

A B L C D E A F T G H X

Y I J O K L U M O R O Z

L Q R I S T G F U H O W

T R Z X S T B H H D I E

F N F G E I O X B O L E

D N F K P O Q F R S Z E

T U X O V W T Y Z H A B

E C F R D E S G H

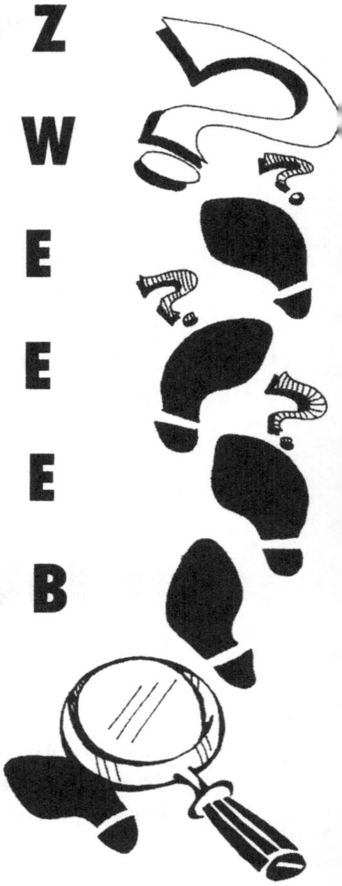

_____

_____   _____

_____   _____

_____

REPRODUCIBLE 13A

Permission granted to photocopy for local church use. © 1999, 2009 Abingdon Press.   ALL-IN-ONE BIBLE FUN

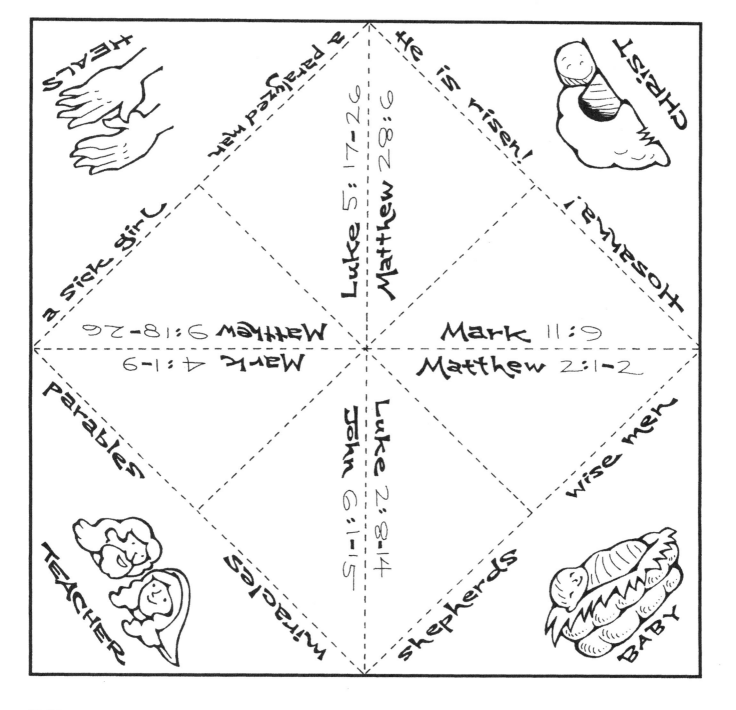

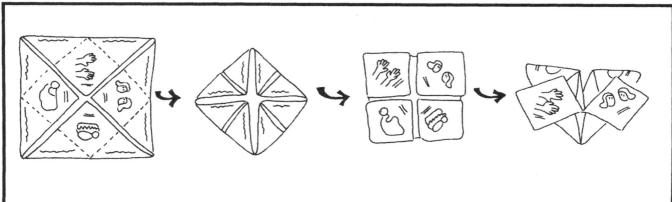

Fruit of the Spirit - Elementary

CPSIA information can be obtained at www.ICGtesting.com
Printed in the USA
LVOW05s0825301214

420807LV00002B/2/P